TAROT PREDICTIONS FOR 12 SUN SIGNS FOR THE YEAR 2023

MONTH-WISE PREDICTIONS FROM TAROT CARDS FOR ALL THE 12 ZODIACS BASED ON SUN SIGNS TO HELP YOU HAVE A FULFILLING YEAR

MEETU SEHGAL

With blessings from Divine Mother and Father

Contents

Foreword

Dear Reader,

Curiosity about what will happen next has driven civilisations to find ways and means to predict the future. It began with star gazing and thus the field of astronomy and predictive art was born. It had its humble origins for the purpose of agriculture and season predictions. But it soon was adapted to predict for humans and their lives.

No matter what kind of predictive art you follow - astrology, numerology, tarot, runes, cartomancy, coffee/tea leaf reading etc. - the purpose of all is to help human beings and individuals live a more satisfying and fulfilling life. But knowing the future is not a guarantee of a peaceful life. Sometimes it can be the opposite based on the dispositions of each individual.

Therefore the best way to use this art form and this book is to take it as a guide to help you deal better with your present, prepare for the future and let go of the past. The fact is that the past is over and it cannot be changed, the future is an imagination and again not real, so the only point of reality is the NOW.

Focus here, how you react to today will determine what comes next in the future. It is after all, about action and reaction or in simple terms, Karma. My prayer is you use this book and the predictions here as a guidance for how to deal with the present and live it in the most satisfying manner.

Grace and Light

Meetu Sehgal

CHAPTER ONE

Overview of the energy of the year 2023

2023 will usher in the energy of personal change for most people. Emotions will run at a high. The upside of this is family connections, love, partnerships. Self-love will hold more importance than anything else.

But self-love is a process which takes time and certain triggers for most people to begin to explore. Personal relationships will hold your attention but a certain lack of sense of self will trigger you into exploring your personal growth and self-love journey as well.

Unpredictability will be a theme that runs through the lives of most people this year. Instead of making any long term plans, it will be better to live in the present and save for the future.

There seems to be an undercurrent of dark forces at play causing destruction and chaos, but it may not be so visible.

Many changes at a global level are foreseen but there is likely to be new beginnings of sorts in the world political situation. Right decisions and actions sometimes feel cruel but they are necessary.

At a personal level too, this will reflect in terms of needing to take the tough decisions that are for the greater good rather than indulge in momentary satisfaction that feels good now but exacts a heavy toll later.

It may feel like spirituality has no place anymore, but being on earth we need to realise that doing our job and taking care of our responsibilities is a spiritual act that is so often underrated.

Entrepreneurship will be at an all time high but only those with solid concrete plans will survive the ups and downs of the world markets this year.

The rampant uncertainty will drive many to seek the soothsayers or as we know them today as astrologers, tarot readers and psychics. Many will also be ushered into taking up spirituality as a major path for themselves.

Always remember, in times of uncertainty, put one foot in front of the other and keep walking. You don't need to stop or be afraid. Life is uncertain. But the changes that nature and mother earth is going through now, they are accelerating and hence the rapid changes produce uncertainty.

Align your heart and mind, meditate, strengthen your intuition and control your impulsiveness.

Numerology of the Year 2023

The year 2023 is governed by number 7.

Numerologically, 7 is the number of Ketu which governs spiritual growth. The significant quality of Ketu or South node in Astrology is that it propels individuals to spiritual growth but often at the expense of material progress. It the heavenly body for detachment.

Ketu in its most primary sense helps you understand and practice detachment. Don't let detachment create a picture of a monk sitting on a mountain top. You can practice detachment in your everyday life as well. Detachment means you enjoy the luxuries of what you have in the present without being attached to them. Attachment creates fear of losing and an attitude of hoarding.

In detachment, we can see the bigger picture and work for the well-being of everyone including the planet. It is our attachments that propel us in greed to hoard objects, money and resources creating an imbalance in the universe. This year will bring opportunities for you to practice detachment.

Tarot correlations for the Year 2023

7 correlates to The Chariot in Rider Waite tarot deck and Awareness in the Osho Zen Tarot deck.

7 is the number of thought, ideas, logic and awakening. Chariot is all about moving ahead, leaving your troubles behind you. But it is also about making a tough choice, especially when you can see the pros and cons of each choice.

This requires awareness and an ability to think clearly. The Awareness card from Osho Zen Tarot is about knowing the truth. This truth can be about yourself, the world, situations or the spiritual truth as well. It is about knowing that whatever action we take, there will be consequences attached - both good and bad.

Present situation is a consequence of past actions. Your future will be a consequence of your present actions. Having the awareness of what action can lead to what kind of results is the beginning of awareness. All that it needs is being aware and more conscious of your thoughts, words and decisions in the now.

This year will provide you ample opportunities to enhance your awareness and not slip into your subconscious patterns of lack and limits.

Monthly tarot predictions for the 12 sun signs for the year 2023

CHAPTER TWO

Aries

March 21–April 19

Overview

2023 will usher in opportunities and new beginnings in many ways. On the personal front this year brings new love, re-igniting passions and good news in existing relationships. Family will be important and you will be involved in family matters in a good way. Professionally though, you may feel as if you need to struggle to achieve your goals and targets. Work environment may not be as you had expected. You may need to make your mark or create stronger boundaries for yourself if you want others to respect you or not treat you lightly. You are likely to be overworked yet finances will be proportionate to your efforts which is a good thing. Make it a point to invest your income and also do a bit of charity to keep the wheel of finances spinning.

First half of the year will be fruitful. Professionally, it will be rewarding. But it will come at the cost of your work-life balance. Fortune favours you, inheritance matters will be decided in your favour, you will benefit from past investments and promotion is likely. This will be a time to firmly establish your roots, create strong foundations for your business or job. You will be more focussed with a certain sense of clarity and purpose. This will be a good time to put your ideas into practice and bring them to life. For students as well, this will be a good time to put in the efforts and reap good results.

Second half of the year will be focussed on family and creating work-life balance. Illnesses like common cold, headaches and sore throat may drag you down but they won't affect your productivity as much. Any investments that you may be planning to make at this time will need thorough examination. Emotionally this will be a fulfilling period. Marriage, childbirth, family functions, pleasant commitments are very likely and they will bring you joy. Overseas travel opportunities will also present themselves to you. Love matters will require your time and attention which you will happily give.

January

Work

The pace of work and professional engagements is likely to be less. But with the Aries temper and fire, it may almost feel like you have stagnated. But that is not the case. This will be a time to take a breather and create strategies for the coming months. Do not try to push through things because they will not happen before its time. New business opportunities from abroad are likely to come to you. However, do not jump into them blindly, do your due diligence because they will be worth considering. You may also experience some workplace conflicts. Deal with them logically instead of letting the tempers flare. Take your time making decisions, you do not have to make them in the moment instantly.

Finances

Financially, this month is likely to be rewarding. You will reap the benefits of your past investments. Loans given out in the past are likely to be returned. A sudden unexpected inflow of money can be expected. But this also comes with caution. Your impulsiveness can also lead you to lose the money you earned very easily. So take your time dealing with your hard-earned money. Avoid any spur-of-the-moment buying or spending decisions as you may regret them later on. This is also a good time to tend to your on-going investments just as a gardener tends to his flowers and plants. You may need to reevaluate investment schemes and options.

Love

Love life may be a little stagnant. You are likely to be very picky about people who you want to spend your energy on. It would be better to choose to wait for the right person to come to light rather than spending your time on anyone who comes your way. If you are looking for marriage, it is good to be practical, but perhaps you are being too practical. Listen to your heart as well. Relationships are not just about mundane things, even though they are very important too. A good marriage or relationship makes you happy, brings you joy and fulfilment. Remember this aspect too. When you meet or interact with someone romantically or as a prospect, ask yourself "Does this person bring me joy and comfort?" Take a decision based on this answer as well.

Relationships

You may experience uncertainty or instability in your existing relationships. It is time to reevaluate some of your relationships. Is the balance of giving and receiving present? Or is one person mostly giving and the other only receiving? There may be hidden agendas that you may sense in certain relationships in your life. Friendships need to be seen through the new lens of your present. Your personal growth may have created some distance or a rift in your present relationships. You will need to find out if that can be repaired or it needs to be let go of. This month will make you rethink your definition of friendships and relationships.

Health

Health concerns may be present but not to the extent that they create problems in your everyday life. Diet and lifestyle will need attention as you may overindulge at times causing your digestive tract and your liver to be burdened. Fasting once a week would benefit your health and mental clarity as well. Pay attention to binge eating and excesses in indulgences. You may not be able to execute your plans for health and exercise very well this month, it will require more effort. A sense of curiosity and creating variety in life will help you towards this end.

Spirituality

You will find yourself too distracted to take a peek within yourself. Family and work will take your time and attention. But it is best not to avoid your inner environment and heal the wounds on the heart from the past.

February

Work

New opportunities are likely to come to you this month professionally. Either a new job or an opportunity from abroad, both are likely. Make a decision keeping in mind the pros and cons. Don't let your fears or resistance from those around you - friends and colleagues - affect your decisions. It may be a big leap in terms of position, area, field or place. Have an attitude of learning as you grow and it will lead you to the right places. Don't base your decision just on the amount of money you earn but also the opportunity for growth and learning.

Finances

A major financial decision related to purchase this month could throw your financial planning into problem. Don't get swayed by emotions or attachment at this point. Keep your wits with you. You don't have to indulge or give in to everyone's demands. You will be able to recover from this. Patience is advised.

Love

Your plans of taking your love relationship to another level may not fructify. Don't lose heart. It is happening for the best. Advice is to take things slow and steady. If you are looking for love, stay in the present, don't make plans too much into the future with a person you just met. Don't wear your heart on your sleeve. Also, you need to heal any past heart breaks in order to manifest a loving relationship. You cannot get into new relationships with baggage from the past. Keep you expectations from your partner practical and you won't be disappointed.

Relationships

Relationships may require your time and energy as unnecessary strains may develop. Sometimes not acting immediately helps in maintaining peace. Clear communication is the need of the hour. Do not let assumptions make home in your relationships with your family. Be willing to give and take some space and time apart to allow love to come in. Your ideas are beneficial for your loved ones. Communicating them in a way that they are perceived as suggestions and not commands is your responsibility.

Health

Health will need attention this month. Back pain, problems with muscles and over exertion can cause issues. Also, do not ignore your mental health. Stress can lead to you catastrophizing situations and creating more anxiety. Seek help, humour will help. Take it easy this month on your body.

Spirituality

You will pay attention to your personal growth this month as circumstances will force you rethink your role in creating and alleviating them. Spend some time in nature, connecting to plants and animals, it will help you deal with your mental health as well as show you the way ahead.

March

Work

Team work will be needed and will produce results this month at your workplace. Do not try to run a one man show as it won't bear the fruits of your effort. However, do not let your ego come in the way of working with others as it will create more problems than solutions. This month will require you to look at the strengths of others and leverage them instead of allowing your insecurities to get the better of you. Do not let any hidden or personal agendas come in the way. Address the elephant in the room before it becomes a problem for all.

Finances

You may find yourself dealing with lack of resources but there is no need to worry as new opportunities for finances will open up creating abundance inflows. Your ideas are good but unless you put them into action, they are of no use. Allow people to contribute and help. Its not such a bad thing. It does not mean you are not good enough, it just means there are people who are willing to help you out when needed.

Love

Good proposals are likely to come your way. You just have to be willing to look. Dynamics with your love partner or your spouse will also improve. But your expectations from them or yourself need to be more realistic. Also, if you are looking for love, you need to make time for it. You can't be too busy to ignore an important aspect of your life.

Relationships

Relationships and family will provide comfort and joy. The troubles may soon be past. Focus on the present blessings instead of getting stuck on the problems of the past. Marriage is on the cards. Enjoy good times with your family and friends. A social gathering is on the cards this month. Personal relationships are also likely to bring in professional opportunities.

Health

Health will be better and support you in your endeavours. Any new plans for a change in lifestyle or health management will be good for you. Don't ignore any signs of bad health. Take action now. Allergies and heart issues need to be paid attention to. Minor changes in food and exercise schedule will be very helpful.

Spirituality

You are a manifestor and have the ability to have the clarity to create what you want in your life. Meditation and slow movement will aid your peace of mind. It is time to face your fears and allow light into your life. Use candles, diyas and more red and orange colours in your life right now.

April

Work

Work this month may be challenging but your sense of will and determination will help you see through any difficult projects. Do not shy away from accepting challenging demands professionally, you are capable of doing it and even helping your colleagues and employees deal with it. Pay attention to those around you who may try to harm you or your reputation. Be careful of who you speak to at your workplace as it can be taken otherwise.

Finances

Finances will be good. New opportunities will come to you easily and your previous investments will bear good results. Stay away from shady schemes for investment or involving your money in other's business plans that are not clear and sound as you could end up losing money. Spend some and keep some for the future is the mantra for the month. You will be able to balance the income and spending with ease.

Love

Love is on the cards this month. Either you will be making proposals or you will be receiving some. Good times spent with your lover or spouse will bring you satisfaction and joy. Marriage is also on the cards, though you may need to make some efforts to be liked by your lover's family or convince your family about it. Remember to keep the give and take equal and not lopsided.

Relationships

A loved one's health might cause you some concern and worry. An addition to the family is likely this month. Father figures will help you deal with difficult situations. You may also be a father figure for someone around you who is ready to become an adult and will need your support and guidance.

Health

Do not ignore your health while you tend to your loved ones. You cannot serve or be helpful if your own cup is empty. There will be many demands on your time but don't ignore your own health in this. You will need to be strict about your lifestyle and not let all the fun affect your diet or health regimens. Headaches this month may trouble you more often. Learn to deal with them in a healthy manner through rest and stress reduction instead of popping pills every now and then.

Spirituality

You might find yourself running or attending to a fast paced life right now so much so that you are likely to not tend to your own spiritual needs. Try snack meditations - 3-5 minutes once or twice a day can also boost your immune system and recharge your batteries. It will also help to keep you grounded and in the present.

May

Work

Opportunities at work will knock on your door this month. But you may be feeling somewhat dissatisfied with what you have been doing. If you have been thinking of switching fields, you might receive offers that may be tempting enough for you to consider. Relationships with colleagues and other professionals will be cordial and help you grow in your workplace. Projects from abroad that you may have been looking forward to can materialise soon.

Finances

Financially this is a good time. You will be happy and content with your money situation. This is not the time to look for avenues to invest or spend. Hold on to your hard earned liquid cash. Be practical with where you are spending your money. It is best not to give out loans to people around you this month.

Love

New love is in the offing. You might receive some interesting proposals but on closer examination they may not be the best especially if you are looking for something long term. In a love relationship, do not fret over little things. Be more flexible. However, do pay attention to your intuitions this time as they are at a high. A chance encounter with someone might turn into something beautiful.

Relationships

You may have been struggling with some of your relationships and wondering if you are getting any value out of those or are you the one always giving. It will be best to confront them sooner than later. Do not lose your sleep over something that can be resolved with a simple communication. You can also choose to create healthier connections by taking charge of the discussions or conversations that may otherwise turn toxic.

Health

Health will be good. Any plans that you have made to improve your health will be implemented easily. Energy levels will be good and will assist you with any lifestyle changes that you may be contemplating. Old health issues will also feel better. If you have been looking for a solution to a health issue, you are likely to find it .

Spirituality

You have been creating too many distractions for yourself so as not to address the chaos happening within. But your dreams are a good indicator of your inner storms. Stop trying to imagine the worst. You are a powerful manifestor. Anything you want you can create with your thoughts right now.

June

Work

There may be a certain sense of instability and uncertainty regarding your work or job this month. Look forward to better opportunities as they are coming your way. You do not have to burn your bridges when you move on to a better project or job. It is all repairable. If you have been thinking of a job change, there is a high possibility of something good coming your way this month. Do not wait for the situation to get worse before switching. Trust your intuition.

Finances

Expenditures may rise this month as you give in your impulses. Remember to take off your blinders and check whatever you are purchasing for its value and utility. You may come across investment opportunities that seem too good to be true. Do your due diligence and do not take decisions just because someone wants you to. Trust your ability to discern the good from the bad.

Love

Your ego battles may put your love relationship at risk. You cannot be right all the time. And remember when you fight with your loved ones and even if you win, it is a hollow victory because both of you end up losing. If you are chasing someone's love, you have to stop and reevaluate if it is worth it. Effort has to be made from both the ends.

Relationships

You may experience changes in your relationships, friendships and the dynamics therein. Do not try to hold to anything, especially not at the cost of going our of your way to do something for someone. Some relationships may be moving out of your life, creating space for some better ones to enter. This process can be confusing and painful but it will be for the highest best.

Health

Health is likely to suffer a bit this month. You may experience back pains and issues with your digestive system. Increase intake of fluids in your diet. You may want to consult or take a second opinion. Any effort you make towards your health this month will reap quick rewards. Moderation is advised in everything you do.

Spirituality

You might find it difficult to centre and calm yourself enough to meditate or do any spiritual work this month. Active forms of meditation and healing will work wonders for you. A chance meeting with an individual will transform the way you perceive life.

July

Work

Changes happening at the workplace might feel uncomfortable and difficult to deal with but they will soon pave way for something better. A move is on the cards, whether it's a shift in the job or location. Remain steady and do not give into emotions at your workplace. Conflicts or showdowns are indicated. You will be able to overcome and come out of it without much damage if you stay steady and use your mind. Do not consult too many people in this phase, trust in your intelligence.

Finances

Finances may bother you a bit this month but its nothing major and long lasting. You may have to factor in your budget and control your expenditure for some time to tide over things. Situation will get better soon so there is no need to worry too much. Just be cautious and careful. Important decisions that you take this month regarding finances will determine your financial situation for some time to come.

Love

You may experience heartbreak and disappointment this month in matters of love. It may feel like the world has ended but it is not so. There is a possibility of recovery from this. Instead of focusing on what went wrong, try to think of what went right, what you could have done better and how you can use this experience to choose better in future. Do seek professional help if needed. You don't have to go through it all alone.

Relationships

Your family and friends are standing strong and steady with you. You need to, however, look at the help they can provide. Be willing to receive the love and assistance with gratitude. It doesn't make you small. It provides you the strength to get up and make your own efforts to create better times. Be open to new friendships as people extend their hand towards you. You may also want to work and heal your patterns of difficult and toxic relationships with a professional.

Health

Health will be average. But the cards do warn you not to overindulge in substances or food. Be kind to yourself and your body, preserve your energy. You do not have to take up any health program that just randomly comes your way. Pick and choose. Find something that's gentle and supportive even for your mental health.

Spirituality

This is not the time to sit still and meditate. It is time to be active, feed your body, mind and soul. Read something new and informative, eat good nutritious food and interact with people who soothe your soul and provide you with a fresh perspective. Learn to look at uncomfortable truths for that is where your growth lies.

August

Work

Work and workplace will demand your time and attention this month as you busy yourself in establishing, taking more responsibilities and managing bigger teams and projects. If looking for a job change, this month brings in the possibilities of finding your dream job. But with your dream job/dream project comes bigger responsibilities. Work-life balance this month is likely to go for a toss.

Finances

Finances will improve as new sources of income open up. If you have been looking for loans, you are likely to receive them this month. Resources will manifest with ease as you become more open to attracting abundance and opportunities in life. A business venture may come up. Look before you leap but it might be worth considering.

Love

You will be open to receiving love and might even explore new dating sites or avenues. Meanwhile keep working on healing your relationship dynamics that haven't worked out in the past. An old flame might show up in your life. Do not jump in with eyes closed as it may cause more trouble than necessary. Work in creating your boundaries even in love.

Relationships

A young one around you is ready to embark on his/her journey. You can mentor someone in your family for their future career or relationship choices. Family and friends will bring joy and fulfilment. You may be consulted regarding a major decision in the family. Don't shy away as your opinion is valued. Marriage or child birth is on the cards. Good news will soon come your way.

Health

Health is improving but anxiety and confusion may still trouble you at times this month. Check on your micronutrients deficiencies. Get a full body check up if you haven't got one done in some time. Do not make hasty decisions about lifestyle changes or some fancy fad diet. It may not do you a lot of good.

Spirituality

This will be a good time to plan a retreat into a quiet and calm place for spiritual work or meditation. It is time to centre your mind, cut through all the unnecessary thoughts and ideas and learn to be in the present. Alternative healing systems might give you a push in the right direction.

September

Work

Workplace situations will move ahead at a pace. This is a time to make quick decisions and be on your feet. There may be some work-related travelling involved as well. If you have been planning to hire an employee or expand your team, this is a good time to do that. It is also time you learnt your lessons from the past and begin to trust your instincts and follow them always.

Finances

Matters of inheritance are likely to be decided in your favour. You may come across sudden inflows of money. If you have been dwelling on a new investment opportunity in an idea, this is the time to take action on it. If you are planning to invest in someone's business idea, make sure you keep close tabs on them to know what's going on.

Love

Do not rush into decisions in the matters of the heart. Take your time, allow the other person to earn your trust and love. Don't fall into the trap of loving someone for who they can be instead of seeing who they are in the present. Everyone has potential, it doesn't mean they will reach there. Choose a mutually loving relationship instead of taking on a project.

Relationships

A marriage or a celebration in the family is on the cards. However, something about your closed loved ones may be causing you sleepless nights and worry. There is indeed more than meets the eye and you do not know everything. But this is not the time to push a conversation. Allow it to happen organically otherwise it won't be a cordial constructive conversation, instead it would become an argument and clash of egos.

Health

Health is doing better than before, yet there may be little things that keep troubling you this month. Do not run away from paying attention to yourself as it could prove costly in the long run. Alternative healing will really help in your health related concerns. Seeking help from a professional for your mental health and stress related issues will be good.

Spirituality

You may want to sit back, relax and have others do the work for you. But that's not how personal and spiritual growth happens. You will need to fight your tendency to take it easy in this area of life and put in your efforts whether it's meditation or some other spiritual practice. Seek our mentorship or support from someone if you are finding it difficult to do.

October

Work

Patience is the keyword this month when it comes to your work. You have sown the seeds and watered the garden, now you must wait for the results to come. Trust the work that you have done. It is time to also start looking at new projects or areas that need your attention instead of obsessing over something that needs time to mature and fructify.

Finances

Finances will be good this month. You will be happy with the inflow of money. You may even end up earning something extra. Do not spend it all away. Rather invest it in your own growth. It may be time to upgrade your skills as well. There may be a financial decision that needs to be taken, however you do not have the complete information yet. It is better to wait than make a hasty decision.

Love

Do not try to rush decisions. Relationships will happen, they will go to the next level but not necessarily at the pace you want. You need to make peace with this fact. Do not jump into a relationship as you may not know everything there is to make a wise decision. Remember to take a look at the big picture, not just what you are feeling in the moment.

Relationships

There have been some relationships that have turned either sour or you have outgrown them. It is time for them to end. But it is also your decision. Choose wisely. You cannot stay in the decision for long. There are new people waiting to enter your life. You need to make space and make peace with the past. If you are waiting for closure with a person, this is the time for it.

Health

Health will be good. If you have been struggling with an illness or health issue, you will find the right doctor or healer for you who will help you get better soon. Meanwhile, do not ignore your own efforts. Don't look for any shortcuts. Whatever you are dealing with, it is almost over.

Spirituality

October will be fairly significant in terms of spiritual experiences. You are likely to see some miracles. Open your heart to love and forgiveness, let go of what is no longer serving you, especially any grief. This is also a good time to start your spiritual journey with a master or guru.

November

Work

The ideas at work that you had been planning or working on may not work out the way you wanted. However it does not mean all is lost. The ideas were good, perhaps you need to re-evaluate its execution. It may also be time to have a constructive conversation with your employee(s) about how you want things done. Your heart is in the right place, you simply need to manage your expectations from yourself better.

Finances

Even though you may experience some loss in an investment, your karmas or your decisive thinking will be able to offset it and save you from losing a lot of money. Stay away from schemes proposed by friends or friendly acquaintances as they may not be in your favour. Better to say No now than be sorry later.

Love

Oh Aries, you and your egos. It's good to stand up for what you believe is right, but sometimes you need to look at others' perspectives too. This month there could be some strain in your love relationship. Don't try to win or lose, instead have a logical conversation about it, exercise patience, as the dynamics of your relationship is changing for the better.

Relationships

Sometimes the solution to people expressing their perspective is just to listen and not to react. That will save you a lot of trouble in your relationships this month. You will be happily involved with your family, perhaps spend some good quality time with your loved ones. If on a vacation, don't try to go to as many places as possible, rather enjoy the moment with your family calmly.

Health

Health will be average this month but moderation is advised. Seek out alternative cures and doctors to help you with your issues. Pay attention to your emotional health as well. Chances are it is causing a major part of what you are going through health wise right now.

Spirituality

This month will teach you to keep your composure even in emotionally distressing situations. A little bit of dedication will help you in following your spiritual goals this month, whether they are daily meditation or Sadhna or some form of learning.

December

Work

Work is likely to flow smoothly this month. Except for the occasional ego conflicts, there will be peaceful times. You will be easily able to handle any office politics with your astute observation and wit. You may even propose ideas that will be encouraged, appreciated and accepted by your colleagues and superiors.

Finances

A financial liability is about to come to an end which has given you sleepless nights for some time now. A loan long due will be paid substantially. If you have been looking for a loan, it is likely to be approved bringing an end to many of your troubles. But this whole process may be taxing mentally. So take care of your mental health and keep a positive attitude.

Love

A new love is likely to enter your life this month. It might be a proposal which may be hard to say no to. But it will come with its own challenges as well. Make sure it is not too much for you to handle. A trip with your lover is on the cards. Plan well so that there are no hiccups.

Relationships

You may want some alone time away from some people in the family. It will do a lot of good if you stay away until the tempers have cooled, otherwise some harsh words may be exchanged which may put the relationship in jeopardy. Children will bring you happiness. A solo trip may be just what you need right now.

Health

You are on the right track for health related concerns. The treatment is working, it's just going to take some time. Some time in nature, whether mountains or beaches, will be rejuvenating for your senses and body.

Spirituality

Even though things may seem ok and calm on the outside, yet there is a storm going on on the inside. It is time to pay attention to the restlessness within. You know you have been making some compromises but you don't have to do them anymore. They are eating away your energy and bringing more sadness to you. Prioritise yourself as you will need all your love and support. Seek a coach or a mentor to help you tide over this storm.

CHAPTER THREE

Taurus

April 20–May 20

Overview

2023 will be about picking up the pieces and moving on powerfully. This year will see you establishing yourself in life in some way. The problems that you have been facing will begin to recede as you figure out ways to rebuild your life again.

Money matters will be of prime importance this year - investing, earning, establishing new sources of income and helping others monetarily as well. Social interactions are highlighted. Your network will expand as more opportunities to meet and interact with people in both personal and professional arenas come your way.

However, stubbornness is also a trait that you have to deal with often in your life. If you are a young person on the threshold of adulthood, you will find your elders or seniors guide you with astute wisdom and clarity. This year is not just about meeting people, but also learning new things from the wise and accomplished around you.

First half of the year will be more about exploring new areas or taking risks. You are open to trusting others for direction and wisdom. However, do not be too blinded by faith or stubbornness. Listen to the wise counsel and do not try to experiment too much. Keep your eyes open and use your sharp intellect and insight to see through the good and bad. The second half of the year will be about experimenting, handling more than you thought were capable of and travel too. It is likely to be hectic and time consuming but it will also read good rewards.

You may even be challenged to move out of your comfort zone to accomplish or learn new things in life. Professionally this year will take up most of your attention and time. Your workplace and your field of work will be challenging enough to keep you engaged yet not so difficult that you are unable to face it. Your patience will be tested but for you Taurean, patience is a virtue that comes from the heavens.

You resonate with the patience element of the Earth where all things take time, results are slow but sure and efforts are ongoing and relentless. This sums up the Taurean energy that you carry with you in every area of life.

Personally this year will bring good rewards and accomplishments. You are likely to find yourself in a stable situation/relationship soon. Married life will be overall peaceful, besides the occasional stubbornness that you express. Personal life will be rewarding and satisfying. Solo trips are on the cards for this year for you.

January

Work

Work and professional life will be satisfactory as you receive positions of authority and responsibility. Your network will bring business for you as well as new opportunities for growth. It is advised to look into business options thoroughly before agreeing to it as not all the options may be good for you even though they all might be enticing enough for you to consider.

If you have been looking for a job, whether a job change or as a fresher, you are likely to land up with a very good opportunity that will help you learn a lot. Your boss or senior may be a taskmaster but they will teach you the practical skills useful to you. This is not the best time to change your field of work.

Finances

Financial situation will be good this month. This might prompt you to spend on get-togethers or on friends. Maintain moderation in this behaviour. The efforts that you have made towards becoming financially secure are finally paying off. It will be a good idea to consult a professional or a wise experienced person for investment related advice. If you are young and just starting out, this will be a good time to begin your investment journey in advice with a father figure or a professional.

Love

Even though many proposals for relationships and love come your way, you tend to think too much into it. Your behaviour in this area of life is at best erratic. Giving all into a connection and then pulling back to think if what you did was right can leave you more confused and hurt the other person as well. Practise patience and move slowly into matters of love. It may be tempting to want to talk or connect all the time but it's certainly not healthy for either person.

Relationships

You will want to and even get to spend good quality time with family. You may not want to do much active work in your personal life this month. Therefore ideally spending some quiet time with your loved ones, going on a spa retreat or a quiet mountainside will be beneficial and rewarding for you and your loved ones. Children will bring happiness and joy.

Health

Health will be average overall. If you have been dealing with a health issue, it is time to get working on it seriously. Half hearted efforts will give half hearted results. Allow others to help you with your health concerns. If you have been dealing with a health issue on your own, it is time to seek professional help.

Spirituality

As healing energy surrounds you, it is time for you to heed the call. If you have been contemplating experiencing or learning an alternative healing system, this is the right time. Your mind is sharp and focussed this month. Practice mindfulness and positive affirmations to help you tide over any challenges.

February

Work

Workplace will provide you inspiration to give your best. You may even enrol in certain courses related to your work that will help further your career and improve your skill set. The only caveat is for you to keep going even if you might want to rest and take some time. This is not the month to delay or procrastinate. Your ideas are good and need further inputs from your mentors to be implemented for success.

Finances

Even though finances won't be a problem this month, yet you may find yourself being frugal with your spending. You are likely to receive a reward or an additional bonus because of your work in the past. It may even come as a gift of money to you. Being careful and minimalist about spending is good but it is ok to spend on yourself once in a while.

Love

You will enjoy some good time with your beloved and may even plan a trip. If you are single and looking, you can be choosy about who you want to spend your time with. But don't keep looking for red flags even if they are not there. It is ok to let yourself relax and enjoy the company of new and interesting people.

Relationships

This is an area of life that will be challenging this month. You may experience disappointment or feel left out in your friend circle or family gathering. This is also a good time to let go of any relationships of convenience and look for something more meaningful. Remember a thumb rule: if you are not happy in a relationship, it is perhaps not the right one for you.

Health

Your health will need attention and care. Unexplained pains or problems may keep you busy this month. Instead of popping pills, try looking into your emotional health. Are you processing and healing your emotional health instead of suppressing your emotions and putting your mental health issues in a closet to be dealt with later? Your body is beginning to scream for help. It is time to address your mind and emotions.

Spirituality

You are ready to embark on a new spiritual path or journey. It may be that you took a break or perhaps you have never looked at this aspect of life. You will receive help in your journey. Look for a mentor who can guide you.

March

Work

Your work will demand all your time and attention this month. You may begin a dream project or perhaps receive the promotion that you have been desiring for a long time. Though the work will come with its own demands, your superiors or clients will be even more demanding. This will require you to put your best foot forward. Any half hearted efforts will just not do.

Finances

This is a time to hold on to your money rather than spend or invest it. Take your time making certain financial decisions. This is perhaps not the best month for that. You may even want to be a bit more careful about keeping your valuables safe this month. Do not share your money plans with anyone this month.

Love

Many opportunities and proposals may come this month. But it might get very difficult to choose between the possible suitors. Avoid taking a spur of the moment decision and consult a wise friend or a family member for their opinion. You do not have to make a decision right away. Take your time, wait for more of their information or character to be revealed. Anything you pursue this month may become a long term association.

Relationships

You may find some distance being created between you and your friends or family members. Or perhaps you will deliberately create the distance so that you can evaluate if that relationship is healthy for you or not. An advice is to not just look at the bad things or flaws but also look at the bright side of the person in question. Everyone has many dimensions. Keep that in mind before you make a decision.

Health

Health is improving but still it needs more care and attention. The efforts that you have been putting in for your body are working. It is the right course of medication or therapy. However, your emotional health still needs more work. You can seek out professionals for help in that area. It will be good for you.

Spirituality

This is a month for transformation. You have been working on yourself and your spiritual journey and it will soon begin to show results. This is a good time to pick up a practice like meditation or breath work to help you go deeper within.

April

Work

This is a time to hold on to your work position or project and not just give it up. You are likely to be presented with alluring opportunities which can tempt you to abandon the wagon but this is not the right time. Do consult experts before making any major decisions. The opportunity may seem very good but in reality it may not be what you expected. So exercise caution. A change of workplace is on the horizon but it is not here yet so hold your position. Work environment will be favourable.

Finances

You will be tempted to invest or spend your fortune on something that may only give you momentary pleasure. A female figure in your life will give you sound advice. Consider that opinion before making any decision. You may also likely be approached by a friend to invest in his/her business or project. Do your due diligence and don't let emotions get the better of you.

Love

Your love life might see some major changes. You may have to experience the agony of a breakup especially if you have been going through a tough time in your relationship or if you have felt as if you are the only one carrying the burden of the relationship. But the good news is that the worst is over. For some of you, this change can also imply tying the knot of marriage or taking your relationship to the next level.

Relationships

In the area of relationships as well, it is time to bring closure to some relations that have outlived their timespan. Don't expect everyone to like you, you do not have to please everyone around you. Cherish the good people you have in your life and let go of those that pull you down.

Health

Your health will be good this month and support you in your day-to-day activities. The worst is behind you. There may still be some health issue lurking that will keep calling your attention, but it's not on the surface yet.

Don't worry about it too much.

Spirituality

Your meditative practices will help you keep your calm this month. The cards suggest an inner child healing will help you in your health as well as spiritual growth. Pay attention to all the times you abandoned yourself, were rude or tortured yourself with words and actions. Make peace with it and accept what happened. This is your time to begin your journey of self love.

May

Work

Your birthday month comes with exciting developments at your workplace. There are likely to be mixed results. A position or job that you had been vying for is likely to slip away from your hands into your competitors'. On the other hand, whatever project you were involved with is likely to bring you success and accomplishments. It will be a matter of mindset whether you look at the glass half full or half empty. There is no threat to your position, you are still secure.

Finances

In your business dealings this month, exercise caution, restraint and compassion too. Look for a win-win situation as any other is likely to bring you empty results. Your networks and old contacts will bring you good news regarding finances. If you have applied for loans or grants, it may get delayed.

Love

The cards ask you to have patience this month in matters of love. Do not jump into any new affairs of the heart especially if you have just gone through a breakup. The rebound relationship can bring more pain than healing. A friendship might blossom into love for some of you. This is not the month for any decisions or major changes.

Relationships

Relationships this month will be particularly fulfilling and bring you hope. A mother figure in your life is there to support you in your tough times. Spend time with teenagers and young adults as it will nourish your mind and bring back your enthusiasm for learning new things in life.

Health

Health will be good. If recovering from an illness, this is a good time to start a new healthier lifestyle. Family will be supportive in your health issues. If you have been thinking of looking for health services abroad, this is the right time to plan it.

Spirituality

The universe is bringing gifts to you. Your manifestation abilities are increasing as you find harmony between your head and your heart. However, your doubts are stopping you from experiencing the magic. Let go of doubts or any deserving issues within you. Affirm to yourself everyday, "I deserve all the good things in life".

June

Work

This month would be about consolidating your position at work and dedicating your time and resources to the job at hand. You will also need to be strict about your boundaries and keep your eyes and ears open about any politics going on around you at the workplace. This month can be challenging regarding your work environment and the people around you. Do not engage in petty politics or gossip as it can hurt you in the long run.

Finances

Finances this month can put you in a difficult spot as your money could get stuck. There could be problems with liquidity and cash flow. Payments might get delayed. But don't worry too much. Your efforts in this direction will cause either an inflow of money from a surprising source or a third party may be willing to lend you the money. In the latter case, be specific of the terms of the money lent, otherwise it might cause you problems in the future.

Love

This month, you could get lucky in matters of love. Some interesting proposals might come your way which you can consider seriously. You will be able to spend some good quality time with your beloved. Plan a mutual interest activity with your loved one as this can help you strengthen your bond and also reignite passion in your romantic life.

Relationships

You are likely to be more decisive regarding your relationships this month as you make the decisions of what's best for you in the long run. You may travel with family for a vacation or an occasion. It will be best to keep things cordial and don't let your egos ruin the family outing. There may be occasional strain in the family regarding who takes the decision or has the final say in matters. Find consensus instead of forcing your opinion on others.

Health

Health will be good. If you have been struggling with matters of fertility and childbirth, you might soon get good news on that front. New diet ideas might just do you a lot of good. If you have been on a weight loss journey, you may begin to see good results. However, health matters are a journey instead of a destination. Don't get ahead of yourself, celebrate the little successes and pull yourself up in moments of failure or weakness. There is no need to be harsh on yourself.

Spirituality

Your intuitions are at an all time high this month as you are in the process of finding the right mentor for yourself. Do not be misled by promises of grandeur or visions of fake spiritualism. Walk your talk, be authentic and make sure your mentor or guru also walks their talk.

July

Work

The workplace can present some difficulties this month as you deal with your increasing workload and a few peers who don't mean well for you. If on the lookout for new opportunities, some good offers are likely to present themselves to you. However, take your time making this decision. Make sure the position and remuneration finally offered will be as per the offer made. There could be discrepancies. If you have been looking for new business opportunities, this month will be beneficial for you. Do the market research before jumping into the wagon.

Finances

Finances will be average. You will also come across new opportunities for making money. If it feels too good to be true, pay attention to the feeling. However, after due diligence if you feel it's a good scheme, go ahead. Investments in stock markets need to be watched closely as you could incur some losses there. Stay away from speculation on money this month.

Love

An old flame could be rekindled this month. Just make sure it doesn't come with any baggage attached, or it may not be worth the effort. Do not blindly fall into love or relationship this month. Understand the difference between infatuation, physical attraction and love. Be cautious of who you interact with. This is not the best month to go out looking for love. Rather spend time with yourself learning a new skill.

Relationships

You may have to experience some disappointment in relationships this month. A close friend or family member may end up behaving in a manner that may seem like a betrayal. But remember to look at the silver lining and the optimistic side as well. Communication can solve many problems and eradicate distances. You still have a lot to cherish in your personal life and many good people who love and support you.

Health

Health will be good. Recovery from an illness will be successful. However, remember the lessons the illness taught you. Some charity work related to medicines and health organisations will be beneficial for you. Be mindful of your food habits and choices. Eat more greens this month.

Spirituality

Everything happens at the right time and in the right manner. We just don't understand or realise it often. Gratitude will help you this month to tide over any difficult times. Remember when the universe closes one door, it opens another. All you have to do is not question why something didn't work, rather look at what will work.

August

Work

Work may feel standstill this month as you weigh your options to move ahead. New opportunities will soon fall into your lap whether it's a new job you had been looking for or a new project or clients that you have been working towards. Do not be afraid to take on challenging work this month as you have more than the required capabilities to see it through. Changes at the workplace may make you feel uncomfortable but change is the only constant of life. Welcome it as it brings new life into your work.

Finances

Expenditures on the family may increase this month. You may even end up making some emotional decisions regarding finances. There may be some worry around money and property matters this month. Pause before you make any major financial decisions. The expenditure can be justified but it still needs some deliberation. Family will be supportive in all financial matters.

Love

You are ready to embark on a new journey in this area of life. A new relationship is on the cards. In existing relationships, the bond will strengthen giving you much joy and satisfaction. You will also be supportive and encouraging for your partner who may need guidance or moral support in their profession. For some of you, you may be taking your love to the next level and making it official as well.

Relationships

Relationships with friends and family this month will be a balancing act as you struggle to please everyone around you. You may be moving away from certain difficulties that have plagued your relationships in the past few months. Get-togethers and a celebration or a social occasion is on the cards this month. Children and loved ones will demand your time and attention which you will be able to give. In this hustle bustle, don't forget to make time for yourself too.

Health

Health will be good as you take active steps towards following a lifestyle or in making good recovery from an ongoing illness. You may have to watch your food habits a bit more closely but you will be able to manage them and be more stoic about what you ingest. You may experience some brain fog or confusion this month as you feel distracted with so much going on. Meditation and walks in nature will help.

Spirituality

Sometimes all you need is to count your blessings and focus on abundance. Universe has blessed you with a lot of goodness and grace and has protected you from harm in many ways. When you count your blessings, the universe brings more of that to you. Get into the habit of journaling.

September

Work

With new work pouring in you may be tempted to charge ahead to work on it and complete it. However, the cards ask you to slow down, take a breath and put your time into working on it. You may need to work on the foundations of it before you start developing it further. Do not take on projects just because you have less work and you want to feel busy or productive as it would be counter-intuitive and create more problems for you.

Finances

Financially this month will be very good as your finances begin to look up. Gains from income are a good possibility. So are new sources of income being added to your present inflow. Property and inheritance matters will likely get resolved amicably. It is time to make use of opportunities as they present to you otherwise it might be too late to make use of them. Overall a good month financially.

Love

Change and patience will be the two keywords that will show up in your love life. An ex might come back into your life. It will be up to you whether to allow them or not. Think from the mind, not the heart in this matter. Remember that people come into your life for a reason, season or lifetime. Know the difference and identify who you would like to keep in your life and who would you like to move on from.

Relationships

Relationships will be overall cordial. You may need to mend a few of them if some strains have affected them. It is important to look at people and relationships from a fresh perspective. People do change, so do situations. You do not have to judge everything from a standpoint of the past. Everyone makes mistakes, so have you. Also remember that you do not have to be close to everyone in the family. A mere acquaintance like relation is also okay with some instead of open hostilities.

Health

Health issues might raise their head again but they won't be as bad as before. Mental chatter might make it seem worse than it really is. speak to a friend or a counsellor to soothe your frayed nerves. Problems with the nervous and circulatory system may trouble you this month. Yoga or any other yin form of exercise will help. Avoid any strenuous activity.

Spirituality

Even though life may seem standstill, yet so much is happening underneath the surface. You do not always have to be active. Just like night follows day, similarly rest follows activity. It is in rest that the body and mind purge the unwanted waste and retain the wisdom, rejuvenating themselves. You are not late for anything. Everything needs time to be nurtured. Give yourself that time.

October

Work

As your work situation improves, you will find yourself with increasing responsibilities as well as having more accountability. Though that may not be a big problem, but there may be some work that may not pass the thorough standards. Don't be disappointed as you still have done a lot of good work. Work related gatherings may take up your time this month. It will be important to groom yourself well as you never know who you may get to meet.

Finances

A loan or debt given to a family member may turn into a bad debt that you may have to write off. However, an old contact or friend may come to your rescue financially and offer you the funds you need to fuel your projects or enterprise. Contacts and networks will be of real value this month. But be careful also of how much you spend on your friends. Spend wisely and be smart so you don't end up paying for everyone else in the group.

Love

You may spend some good quality time with your lover this month. Perhaps even a vacation is likely. It will help you break away from the routine and renew your relationship as well. If you have recently gone through a break-up, it is recommended to get some help or therapy to get over the excessive thoughts about your ex that may be bothering you. You need to find closure or give one. Face the situation instead of distracting yourself from it.

Relationships

You may experience a loss of a relationship this month. Your family will be quite supportive of you during this time and will help you tide over the tough time. Acknowledge the care and nurture that your family provides for you. Often that goes unnoticed or unacknowledged. Advice from an elder around you will help you in some crucial matters in your life.

Health

As the season changes, you may experience some health related issues. But timely action and healing will make sure you are fit and fine in no time. Health problems related to coldness or an imbalance of heat and cold in the body can cause you to feel dizzy, make you susceptible to cold, chest congestion or something similar. Take proper precautions.

Spirituality

You are encouraged to dive deeper within yourself and connect with your own healing energy this month. Perhaps learning any alternative healing methods might be helpful. If you are looking forward to starting your own healing business, this is the time to gain more wisdom about it.

November

Work

Work opportunities or the inflow of work may slow down this month which may be cause of worry for you. You may also have to deal with work related issues or problems at the workplace which will take up a lot of your time. Don't be afraid to seek help as it can pull you out of a tight spot. Have control over your words as they could cause more trouble, this is a temporary phase and will soon pass. Don't let this stress affect your health or work.

Finances

Be wary of lending money to anyone this month as it may never come back. You may experience some loss in your investments as well. Avoid investing in partnerships or a venture of your friend's. This is a month to hold what you have, guard your finances against unnecessary losses and expenditures. Avoid any expenses that are not completely necessary or important.

Love

You may find yourself being a bit too stubborn in your love relationship which may cause a rift between the two of you. You don't have to be in charge always to make things work. You are in a partnership, treat it as an equal one. Your wanting to take charge of your life could lead you to shutting your partner off. Don't do that, allow them to support you during this time.

Relationships

As your relationships undergo a degree of change, you may have to choose between one or more people which may turn out to be very difficult. You may need to make efforts to create peace or some amount of cordiality in between family or friends, but do not side with anyone.

Don't get involved in other's conflicts or it will cause problems for you. A marriage in the family is on the cards.

Health

Health will be fine this month. You may experience elevated levels of stress and uncertainty in life which can cause you to have lowered energy levels this month. A sedentary lifestyle is not recommended. Keep yourself active mentally and physically to keep your health in good shape.

Spirituality

The night is darkest before dawn. Don't lose hope. Don't allow yourself to speak negatively. Every word you speak or every thought you think is a prayer into the universe. Make sure you remember this and use your power of intention to create the blessings. Don't give your power away to time. How you conduct yourself in times of distress determines the quality of the coming days.

December

Work

Work this month will be good as new opportunities are likely to pour in. Your network and extended family might bring in options. You may also receive some communication from people with whom you have worked in the past. It will be pleasant and bring some good news for you. Be particular about avoiding any involvement personally with people from your workplace as it could lead to problems.

Finances

A new financial opportunity can come your way, perhaps in the form of a business proposal or an investment scheme. Though they may be good ideas, yet do your due diligence, research the ideas or the opportunity and only then invest your money. Any loans that you had been waiting to be sanctioned may get delayed putting a damper on your plans. But it's a delay not a rejection.

Love

You will need to create a deeper connection in your existing love relationships. Perhaps spending a day with your partner doing something that both of you enjoy, an activity that stimulates the mind as well could serve that purpose very well, like adventure sports or a painting class. If you are looking for love, then this is perhaps not the time to compromise or settle with whoever comes your way. There is more to love than just the love chemicals. Keep that in mind while choosing a partner for yourself.

Relationships

A happy addition to the family is on the cards. A childbirth or marriage or a similar celebration is likely to bring more joy in your life and bring the family together as well. Plans for a long awaited trip or a vacation could fructify now. A mother figure around you will play an important role in your life. Heed to their advice.

Health

Health may need some care as you have overworked yourself and may feel the burden of the responsibilities on your shoulders. Spend some time in nature or alone in your favourite spot to rejuvenate your energies. It is ok to take a break once in a while. Problems with digestion may cause you some trouble this month. Paying attention to your food intake will be helpful. Remember to practice moderation.

Spirituality

You will need to make a choice in a long-awaited decision. No matter what you choose, it will bring about spiritual growth for you. Remember, not choosing is also a choice that will bear its consequences. Your growth and understanding are unfolding at a great pace right now and you feel more connected than ever to your soul, gifts and purpose.

CHAPTER FOUR

Gemini

May 21–June 21

Overview

2023 will be a year when co-operation, working with others, partnerships in both professional and personal life will be highlighted. You will be engaging with more people, reaching out to them for both personal and professional reasons.

This is a good year for those who are in sales and business development or in professions where you need to interact with people directly. Professionally you will find avenues to establish yourself and create strong foundations for your career growth. Personal life will be demanding as well.

You will spend more time with family.

This is also a year when you will be spending time and resources on upgrading your skills, pursuing higher studies as well as professional qualifications. You may also find yourself and your life under scrutiny from your close relatives that may feel intrusive but also make you more aware of your own habits and lifestyle.

This year is likely to be a wish fulfilment year as all the things that you have wanted and worked for are within your grasp. You are also likely to work on your own self, enhancing your meditative or any other spiritual practices that you are inclined to. This year highlights the feminine aspect of you making you caring, nurturing and trying to create harmony in your environment. As a result, your intuitive senses and empathy will also be heightened helping you connect with your loved ones on a deeper level.

The first half of the year will be focussed on work and consolidating your position at work and in business. Social gathering will also take up much of your time but will be enjoyable. As a Gemini, you are in your true element when surrounded with people and engaging in a battle of wits. You will get plenty of opportunities for such an endeavour.

The second half of 2023 will be a bit tough on you as you wade through some disappointments in personal life or from people that you consider close to you. This will be a time that teaches you trust, expectations, value of friendships and your ability to trust your gut instinct. Although you are pretty good at listening to your instincts, however, following them is sometimes where you slip up.

Overall, this year will be a mix of successes and a few disappointments. You will spend a lot of your time surrounded by people. So it is advised to take a break from social life once in a while to gather your energies.

January

Work

Work will be slow but challenging this month as you struggle to solve some complex issues and find solutions to long-pending problems. Resources will be at your disposal and colleagues as well as superiors will be supportive of you. Do not let some setbacks make you give up on your dream. Persistence will yield good results in your business. You still have a lot going on for you even if what you have is not exactly what you expected.

Finances

Finances will be steady. Any grants that you had been waiting for are likely to be approved this month. Even though the income may be steady and good, yet hidden or unexpected expenses may find their way into your life. Consulting a professional to manage your money may be a good idea this month. Instead of trying to prove your worth to someone else about how much you earn, being satisfied in yourself and with what you have will be more helpful and give you the much needed peace of mind.

Love

In matters of love, this is a fortunate month. If you have been looking for love, you need to make sincere efforts in that direction. Hard hearted efforts and only ideas don't make any difference. If you are in a committed relationship, perhaps it's time to make it official and take it to the next level. If you have been recovering from a heartbreak, you will receive the much needed closure.

Relationships

Even though you may think you are better than others when it comes to intelligence, however, trying to prove that point with close loved ones is a recipe for disaster. Even if you win, you end up losing a cherished relationship or a friendship. Have patience, not everyone can think as fast as you can. Give them time to process the information. A father figure close to you will be helpful and support you in your efforts and adventures.

Health

Health will be good and will support you in all your endeavours. If you are recovering from an illness, this month will bring in some good news. Any new health programs that you may choose to begin this month will yield good results and you are also likely to be consistent with your efforts.

Spirituality

Sometimes we are faced with choices of letting someone in in our life or letting someone walk away. Either if the choices are difficult but we need to remember everything has its own time and happens in its own time. All we need to do is put one step in front of the other and keep walking ahead. Trust in divine wisdom and divine timing.

February

Work

Work will be better this month compared to the last one. Even though new projects and growth will happen, but the progress will be slow which can be frustrating. But this is not the time to be aggressive. Making investments in important areas of business will yield good results in future. So don't not postpone that. Moderation in your approach to work and clients is advised. Do not try anything risky this month as it could backfire. When making any hiring decisions, take your time and do thorough competency checks.

Finances

Finances will be average. There is a possibility of some money getting stuck in a venture or blocked from a vendor. Make your plans accordingly. A celebration at work or home may throw your budget off track. Nurture what you have. Don't intend to invest every penny into one investment basket. Keep some liquidity with you to meet urgent financial needs as they arise. Be cautious of lending money to someone as it may not come back in the expected time period. Also check to see if the money will be actually used for the purpose stated when lending.

Love

Love relationships will be good and fulfilling. Find hobbies or activities of mutual interest with your partner and engage in them. It will help you keep the spark in your relationship alive and even re-ignite the passions. Intimacy is not just physical but also intellectual. Bear that in mind when engaging with your love interest. If you are seeking love, you are likely to meet someone as exciting as you expect. They are likely to be a good match for you.

Relationships

This month will challenge you into making some effective changes in the way you relate to people. Relationships are a matter of heart. Using too much of your intellect and mind can sometimes hamper them to an extent of breaking them off or hurting the other person. Keep that in mind especially as you engage with extended family and your friend circle. A relationship doesn't have to be a battle of wits. Avoid being stubborn in your relationships. Choose better means of communicating your thoughts.

Health

Health will be good. New ideas related to health and fitness need to be tested before implemented completely in your life. You could also consult an expert in this matter. If you have been battling a health issue or working on weight management, begin to study the root cause instead of trying to fight it away. Addressing the root of a problem will give you the required results soon.

Spirituality

Life can be a balancing act. Sometimes the balance has to be between thinking and doing. If you have been doing a lot of thinking as against doing off late, you need to reevaluate the balance. Plans without action are just that - plans. Do the work -meditate, workout, practise your craft or whatever it is you do. But do it, don't just think about it.

March

Work

Work will be good this month as you find yourself juggling multiple projects or businesses with ease. Some new ideas may be proposed to you. They may provide good returns in the future but still need a thorough look into. Partnerships will be good for you. Your business partner and colleagues will be supportive and trustworthy. This will be a good time to begin a business in partnership. You may have to work part time along with your business to support yourself financially for some time to come.

Finances

Finances will be good. If you have been planning to sell a property, you are likely to get a good return on it. This is also a good time to invest in real estate. Caution is advised in financial matters especially related to investing in someone's business or in a venture supporting your business. Do not jump into any such matter blindly. Take a look at the big picture and future plans and vision before making any major financial decisions.

Love

A relationship may become official. Marriage is on the cards. There may be an issue with the approval from family but it would get sorted out soon. A person from past may show up in your life, perhaps a friend or an ex, in hopes of turning the relationship into something more intimate. Do what your instinct says is right. You will be able to spend some good time with your loved one.

Relationships

If you have been running away from certain relationships, this is the time to stand and face them. You may be called upon to play the role of a father figure as a guide or a mentor for a young one around you who is ready to step into adulthood. You may even be helping someone in the family with professional matters. There is a possibility you may be involved in the planning of an event in the family. You will have to pitch in your time and efforts into running some errands.

Health

Health will be average. You may experience some tension in muscles in the back or in legs at times this month. Consult a therapist if the pain persists for more than a few days. Your efforts into improving your health and recovery from an illness are bearing fruits. Any progress is good progress no matter how slow. Acknowledge it and celebrate it.

Spirituality

You will be attracted and called to learn some form of alternative healing system. It will provide a stimulus to your spiritual growth and also give you the opportunity to serve others through healing them. Serving has always attracted you and this will be an excellent place to begin. Follow the moon cycles to regulate your moods and spiritual practices.

April

Work

Work will be satisfactory as some projects come to an end and new projects also get lined up. An enhancement in profile or position is indicated. Bear in mind any enhancement comes with additional responsibilities. Some subordinates might give you a tough time this month. You may have to be diplomatic in resolving the issues that crop up with them. Instead of looking at the situation from a winning or losing perspective, look at how you can work in cooperation and harmony.

Finances

Finances this month may be a source of stress. There is a likelihood of losing some investment or going into bad debt. So be cautious while lending out any money. You may also have to do a thorough check of your account books to check if everything is in order for the new financial year. You will be able to move away from any financial problems towards the end of the month.

Love

This month is hopeful regarding love relationships. If you have gone through a break-up or are still considering if you should or not, cards suggest you to hope for the best and make a decision. The longer you delay the more painful it is likely to get. If you have had a breakup recently, no matter what you think you want, a new relationship is likely to come your way sooner than you think. Maybe perhaps even a patch up is possible. So don't lose heart.

Relationships

Friends and family will be a source of happiness this month. You are likely to find yourself in family get-togethers interacting with relatives. It may even be a celebration in the family. You may be celebrating a young one's good result or an achievement. Overall, this is a good time to get in touch with those whom you had lost touch with. Overall, the atmosphere will be peaceful.

Health

Health will be average. Health checkups are likely to yield good results. Minor problems with digestion or inflammation are likely to bother you this month. If you have allergies, you will need to be prepared or practise preventive measures. A good physician might be able to direct you to the right course of action for any ongoing illness which will benefit you.

Spirituality

You will be able to connect with the right healers and mentors for your spiritual concerns. Receiving and giving healing sessions will benefit you karmically as well. Never assume you know everything, there is always so much more to learn. Be open to receiving. You may also become a mentor or guide for someone else who is beginning their journey in the world of spirituality.

May

Work

If looking for a job change, new offers are likely to come your way but they may not be what you had been expecting. It is imperative that you reassess your capabilities. Perhaps adding on to your skills by doing relevant learning courses will be good for you. Many changes are happening at the workplace that may feel uncomfortable. But they are not all that bad. There may be a change in your office structure or the hierarchies. Take it in your stride instead of resisting it. Stay away from bad-mouthing anyone at the workplace even in the guise of fun as it could backfire.

Finances

Finances will be good. However, out of the blue expenses may throw you off guard and disrupt your plans. But the disruption won't be significant. Holding liquidity more than required is not a good idea. Find out good avenues for investment and consider them seriously. You may be presented a business opportunity or perhaps you have been thinking of one which will require considerable investment. Think through the plans carefully and then go ahead.

Love

Matters of heart will bring you much joy and contentment this month. You can plan the long pending road trips with your partner. It will help you deepen your relationship and also help you explore some hidden gems. If you are looking for marriage, this is an auspicious month. However, finding time for relationships could be a challenge. But it is something you will need to take time out for and put in your efforts.

Relationships

Relationships will be a mixed bag this month. Some people in the family may feel like an enigma or behave in an unpredictable manner forcing you to re-evaluate who you can trust or confide in. You may also have to change the way you approach relationships and friendships. Understanding clear boundaries between acquaintances, relatives, family and friends will save you from a lot of drama. Some people in the family may end up disappointing you. Do not take it to heart. Instead learn from it.

Health

Health will need attention this month. You have been working more than your capacity which has elevated stress levels. If you have blood pressure related issues, this will be a time to keep tabs on it closely as it could give you some problems. Be open to accepting help from others as it will ease your burdens and also give you additional insights into the causes of your health problems. Seeing an expert will benefit you in understanding the root cause of the issue and adopting a more holistic approach to health.

Spirituality

Advice for healing is coming up repeatedly for you therefore pay attention to the signs and sign up to learn a natural or alternative energy healing system for yourself. If you are already trained in it, this is the time to Start practising it for yourself for health or any other challenges you may be facing. Avoid procrastination or sweeping the problems under the rug. It is only going to create more difficulties for you.

June

Work

Partnerships in business or at work are likely to be collaborative and supportive. Your network will yield good business for you. If you are moving on to a new organisation or to a new project, it is advisable not to burn your bridges. There will be a cordial atmosphere between your colleagues, superiors and subordinates. You are likely to receive many good offers for job or business opportunities. But before you choose any, it is advised to look into all carefully not just from a business perspective but also from the human perspective and work environment and only then make a decision.

Finances

Financially this month will bring in new opportunities for investment and growth. If you have lost any money in the past in a venture, this month will help you recover that lost money through new sources. You may also be called upon to learn a new skill set related to managing money. Things are likely to go in your favour this month as what you want happens in the manner you want it. Count your blessings and open your heart and mind to abundance.

Love

Love matters will take up time and attention this month. You will be involved with your loved one and would want to do business or engage with them in a professional capacity. But the lines between personal and professional will need to be drawn very clearly otherwise they may produce more problems in your personal relationship. If you have recently gone through a breakup, you are likely to receive a loving gesture. Do not ignore love as it enters your life.

Relationships

Relationships will be fulfilling and satisfying. Get-togethers and a vacation with the family is on the cards. You may be engaged in helping people in the family with some professional or legal matters. Do not make their issues your own. Keep the required distance when doing so. Also you will need to discern what to share with whom this month. It is advised not to share everything with everyone because some may misunderstand your actions or gestures.

Health

Health will be average. You will be worried about quite a few things especially regarding your health. But losing sleep over such matters is not recommended. Health problems are not as bad as you imagined. Fasting on new moons and full moons will be helpful for your health and mind.

Spirituality

You are being called upon to heal yourself and others through your words and actions. Practice kindness and share your love with the world, even with those whom you deem undeserving. Health will respond to chakra balancing and healing the heart chakra especially.

July

Work

Work will be good as you establish your stronghold in your place of work or your career. This is the month to take stock and check your inventories. Those in desk jobs may be involved in quite a bit of paperwork. This is also a time to begin planning for new projects as the work will begin soon and you may not get enough time then. Any work related problems that were present due to money issues are likely to get resolved this month.

Finances

As finances flow into your life, new expenses also mount up. But you are not likely to feel the pinch. A bad investment may create some disappointment and you may need to change your plans for the near future. Be flexible enough to do that now as being rigid about this won't help. Patience is advised in matters of money, finance and loans.

Love

Even though you may want to carve your heart out for someone you love, your mind is active enough to help you see any reason or logic in the situation. Listen to the voice of reason. You don't have to sacrifice yourself just to gain love. Otherwise, love matters will be satisfying and bring you joy and good times.

Relationships

Your attitude towards relationships will need to be more practical this month. Avoid over promising or getting involved with some people who may not bring any joy and be a complete waste of time. You may have to tread lightly around certain relationships lest you create more problems there. A close friend will help you and guide you in certain tricky situations. Listen to that.

Health

Health will be good. Your efforts will yield better results provided you follow through the instructions. You may begin something with a lot of zest but it could fizzle out soon, so maintain the pace. This month you may experience problems related to increased heat in the system causing skin problems, acidity, increased blood pressure or inflammation. Avoid temperature extremes.

Spirituality

Many things in your life that you may have struggled with are likely to receive resolution bringing your life in harmony. Your thoughts in this direction will provide a great impetus to this. Harmony begins inside, and then is reflected in the environment. So strive for it by meditating, relaxing and listening to peaceful music or chants.

August

Work

As new opportunities for work and business arrive, you may be left wondering and in awe of how the universe works. Allow yourself to make complete use of those opportunities as they may not knock your door twice. There is no use brooding over opportunities lost and people who have moved out of life. New hirings will soon begin opening up a world of opportunities for you.

Finances

Finances may come at a stand still this month as some money gets blocked and payments are delayed. However, do not worry too much as this is just a temporary phase. You may have to make some efforts at your end to make things flow again. Stay focussed and don't let money worries cloud your judgement.

Love

A new relationship is on the cards especially if you have been trying to manifest a new beautiful relationship. Don't get stuck on your ideals or expectations too much as they don't seem realistic enough at this point. They were perhaps made by you so you don't get hurt in love, but these walls will end up hurting you more. Go out, meet new people and if you are in a relationship, spend time with that special someone.

Relationships

This month is more about focussing at the right place instead of the past which is over. Supportive people and friends are around you if only you are willing to look and recognise them. A mother figure around you will be loving and caring and will help you make some tough decisions as well. Cherish the bonds you have, forgive those who hurt you because life is beginning to move forward. Embrace it.

Health

Health will be good as you make efforts and spend some time everyday looking after yourself. A recovery from an illness is on the cards. You may even have to look for a second opinion for certain health problems. You cannot expect others to always take care of you, you need to make those efforts for yourself on your own if you want to see the results.

Spirituality

You may feel as if the universe is not listening to you or not paying attention. The reality is far from it. Universe is always listening, it is just us who at times stop listening and noticing the signs. This month, notice the signs the universe and your angels send you, ask for them if need be and renew your faith. You are always being looked after. Remember the universe is unconditional. God is not a fear based entity out there to judge and punish you.

September

Work

Work this month will be fast paced. Yet you are advised to maintain a certain pace otherwise you may feel exhausted soon. A forward movement in projects and ventures is indicated. Any obstacles will be taken care of. This will be a good time to connect with people in your workplace or in your network. Get to know them before asking for work. Creating work-life balance will be difficult but you will be able to manage it with some effort.

Finances

Finances will be good. Your investments are going well. So if you were planning to make some changes, this is not the right time. Things are likely to go according to plan. You may need to consult a financial advisor this month to chalk out plans for the future. Avoid making any risky investments in business proposals until you are fairly sure it's worth it. Do not be misled by lofty information. Read the fine print.

Love

There may be some uncertainty and confusions regarding personal relationships. You are likely to meet someone interesting this month and things could turn into a passionate affair. Caution is advised. Don't take things too fast. Pace yourself. Spouse hunting will be fruitful this month. But don't get too obsessed about anything or anyone. Let this be a part of your life, not your complete life.

Relationships

Look at the bright side of things this month. You may feel left out or alone as a certain invitation that you had been expecting is not extended to you. But it may just be a mishandling rather than a deliberate intent. Be playful in your personal relationships this month. There is no need to take anything too seriously. A playful attitude will help you get along with almost anyone that you meet in family gatherings. Have fun.

Health

Your health may not be what you expected but it is not bad either. Recovery from any long-standing illness is happening at a slow but sure pace. Try to stick to your regular lifestyle and make it a bit more healthier. There is no need for any drastic shifts in matters related to health. Avoid any form of excesses this month as it may not sit well with your body right now. Keep a close eye on your liver health.

Spirituality

When the universe offers, receive it with gratitude. Resistance is in the mind when we feel we are not deserving enough to receive any good things or joy in life. Whereas, we are meant to experience everything on earth, including sadness and happiness. So stop resisting and take the help if needed.

October

Work

You may hit a few roadblocks at work this month as you struggle to make the best decisions. It is suggested to face and look at all the facts before choosing any options. If you have been looking for a job change, this is perhaps not the right time as the opportunities coming up are not as per your calibre or expectation. Take your time, do not try to run away from any problems whatsoever. Seek advice from a mentor who will happily guide you towards the best course of action.

Finances

Financial situation is likely to be comfortable this month. Money matters will need your attention as you may want to look into alternative investments or expanding your portfolio will be a better idea. Matters of inheritance will be settled without much problems. Money making opportunities from abroad can materialise if you have been working on this.

Keep your head over your shoulders and make decisions calmly.

Love

If you are in a relationship, avoid the temptation to seek out love outside your commitment as it will only lead to more heartache. If you feel the spark in your existing relationship has died, work towards re-igniting passions instead of turning away from it. Spend time with each other alone as well as in company with friends and family. It will help you rekindle the love and remind you of the bond you have shared with this special person.

Relationships

Relationships may go through some turbulent phases this month. Intentions of certain family members or friends may not seem clear enough, listen to your instincts and work according to it. Avoid difficult relationships as much as possible if you want them to survive as proximity could trigger old problems. Avoid engaging in any arguments, sometimes avoiding the problem is a better solution than always facing it and creating more unpleasantness.

Health

Health will be fine. Listen to the sound advice being given by your doctor or a wise family member. Try to engage in activities outdoors so that you don't go too deep into your shell. Staying alone this month can create more mental health issues. So seek out friends, or a therapist. Meet new people, or just go out and interact with someone.

Spirituality

Plenty of changes are happening right now at many planes of existence. Do not try to be too hard on yourself now as you are going through a phase of transformation and change. This is the time to actively assist yourself to go through this change process by taking steps towards your own wellbeing. Take time out to meditate, read, listen to uplifting stories and do some inner work.

November

Work

You may experience a certain level of inertia this month at work. You may be procrastinating or indulging in activities that are unproductive. Get focussed this month on your goal, look at the big picture. Or perhaps find a goal that inspires you and motivates you to wake up in the morning. A partnership may be offered to you. It may be a good deal but do check the fine print and the real potential in the deal.

Finances

Financially, this is likely to be a good month. There may be some expenditures on luxuries or purchases of a car or a house. You may have to create a balance between the income and expenses as it might get a bit difficult this month. Don't let your emotions get the better of you. Follow your ideas but don't think too long term right now. Stay in the present about your financial matters and don't count your chickens before they hatch.

Love

This month may be a little tough in matters of love. You may be disappointed with someone's behaviour whom you had been considering seriously as a partner. Perhaps it is time to create realistic expectations. Make sure you are not projecting someone else's beliefs or expectations on your partner. Take the middle road, don't engage in any extreme behaviour.

Relationships

You are on your guard with respect to certain relationships in your life. It's not a bad thing but it is also very exhausting to be in this mode always. It is better to find strategies to deal with a difficult individual in the family rather than working from a place of fear. Friends will be supportive and help you deal with the situation better. If you have been thinking of moving away from your family home, it may not be possible this month but it is not a bad idea.

Health

Health will need care but the worst is behind you. Any injuries that you have been nursing will show signs of healing this month. Though you will still need to tend to them. A new approach to healing can work wonders, so don't be afraid of exploring alternative healing systems. Progress is assured. You may take some time getting started on any health programs but once you begin, you will progress quickly.

Spirituality

You have a lot of inner strength which perhaps even you are unaware of. This is time to tap into that strength so that you don't get disheartened again so soon. Build an inventory of your capabilities and your blessings and read them out when facing bleak times. Remember, at any given moment, no matter how bad the situation is, there is always something to be grateful for. Focus on that.

December

Work

The work may not be moving at the pace you like this month. The new job or projects are going to take some time to materialise. Meanwhile, tend to what you have at present and don't keep worrying about what's not here. Take some time to build or nourish your network and make new connections. This is the time to do the networking that is required in your field of work. Don't try to find work to fill your vacant hours as it would be counterproductive.

Finances

Finances will be good. But no matter how hard you try, the changes or growth or any other financial matters you want to deal with won't move faster than you want or in a way you like. But the good thing is that there is growth on the cards. Take time to review your investments, build up on new plans and prepare a blueprint on how to execute them.

Love

Your intimate relationship will need some work as you may sense some distance between you and your beloved. It is time to have open communication with the intent of finding a solution instead of blame games. If there are issues in your relationship or marriage it is advisable to address directly instead of finding other avenues outside. It is possible to renew your relationship, work on the issues and be open about sharing the real problems.

Relationships

Some of your relationships may disappoint you, though all is not lost. Yet it may feel like it is over. The lack of trust will be difficult to deal with. However, this is a time to really look into your priorities and find out what you want from each of your relationships. Are your expectations real? Are the people whom you are expecting from capable of giving you what you want? It is necessary to do some soul searching and then make a clear decision about your priorities.

Health

Health will be good. You are likely to hear favourable news about an illness that you have been dealing with. It is time to celebrate the progress. At the same time, do not become too complacent as well. There is still more work to do. Any health plans will come in as a breath of fresh air. Embark on the journey with good faith and optimism.

Spirituality

You might experience a crisis of faith this month. But remember it is just a process to help you learn and grow. Lessons sometimes are not easy. They shake the whole foundation upon which we have build our life. But they are reminders of times and incidences where we went wrong, either we didn't listen to ourself or we ignored red flags that we could clearly see and yet doubted ourself. Take these experiences as lessons instead of deeming them as punishments or injustice.

CHAPTER FIVE

Cancer

June 22–July 22

Overview

2023 will be a year of awakenings. Changes are on the horizon in both personal and professional aspects of life. As you charge ahead with many plans and ideas, you are likely to face situations that will force you to re-think and re-adjust your strategies. Therefore it is recommended to not plan too much ahead into the future. It is best to have a sense of direction and go with the flow.

Spiritual awakenings will be abundant. If you have been working towards your spiritual growth, this will be a pleasant change. But if this catches you by surprise, it may feel overwhelming to deal with. Seek out help through mentors, guides and gurus. You are likely to meet one this year who will propel you ahead in your soul journey.

This is a year when a new course of study will be alluring and you are likely to learn new skills. Seek out courses that inspire you, learn about things that you have always been interested in. You may also be involved in doing professional courses to enhance your career prospects in the future. A break from the past is indicated. You may have to process grief over what is lost. But you are more than ready to move on.

Personal relationships will teach you humility and you will learn how to create balance between heart and mind so as to create healthy boundaries in your relationships of all kinds. Professionally, this will be a year of progress and growth. Many hurdles from the past will move out of the way paving a successful road ahead.

First half of the year will bring in many opportunities for work as well as in personal life. You will also reach out to people for help, business partnerships or even personal relationships. You will be working hard and relentlessly. The second half of the year will be more about taking time, patience and looking before you leap. You will be required to wait and rest. Life will seem to move slowly but in the background many developments will be happening.

January

Work

New job offers or partnership offers are likely to fall into your lap this month. You will be in a good state of mind that will be conducive for you to undertake major projects. There may not be any major progress on the work front but quite a few events will take up your time and attention. Mingle at the workplace, get to know the people as they could provide a more efficient environment at the workplace.

Finances

Finances will not be as bad as you imagine. Instead of worrying about upcoming expenditures, focus on finding solutions. You may be able to clear some of your debts this month. But still a tight reign over finances and expenses will help you ride through any tough spots. Things will work out, outcomes are likely to be favourable, so instead of getting stressed about the future, stay optimistic and affirm a positive outlook for abundance.

Love

You may experience some problems in matters of love this month. Stay away from fleeting love or infatuation, rather stay away from indulging in it as it is likely to create difficulties for you. Be honest about your intentions in relationships, especially with people you meet this month. You may experience a disappointment from a loved one that could lead you to reevaluate that relationship specifically or relationships in general.

Relationships

Family and friends will be a source of comfort and support. When interacting with family, especially extended family, you do not have to like someone to talk to them, have a neutral discussion instead. Don't be too involved in work that you ignore your loved ones. Find time for your family and friends too. There may be a rift between you and a friend. However, it's not that big to not try to repair the connection.

Health

Health will be average. You are likely to stumble across a health diagnosis that might shift how you see health and lifestyle. You may have to spend some time searching for the right solution but with your diligence and intuitive capabilities, you are likely to find it sooner than later. Stay away from cold foods and drinks as they may create an imbalance in the body. Pay attention to any underlying emotional factors in health issues to find a cure.

Spirituality

You will be required to do the work on your personal growth and emotional wellbeing this month. Your persistence and patience will be well rewarded. This may involve seeking out a guru or a mentor who can help you undertake the journey of spiritual well being that lies at the heart of your physical well being.

February

Work

This month will bring in fresh opportunities and growth prospects. A significant achievement is indicated at the workplace. There may be some rift between your employees or subordinates that may cause some trouble for you but it's not something you won't be easily able to deal with. You are in a powerful position this month. Your empathy and leadership skills put you in the right position for your job. Overall, this will be a satisfying month.

Finances

Finances will be good this month. Your past efforts will bear fruits as you receive the desired compensation for a job well done. Some projects are coming to a close and any stuck payments are likely to be received this month. There may be some delays and hurdles as you try to move ahead at a fast pace. Have patience, things are working out in the right manner at the right time. All the resources you require will be at your disposal soon.

Love

In matters of the heart, this month may bring some mixed results. The pace of the relationships will be fast, you will be able to spend some good quality time with your partner. But if you are looking for love, this may not be a very favourable month. You may have to face rejection or being ghosted. But don't lose heart. The right person will come into your life soon. What is required of you is to be more clear and practical about the kind of person you want and then become that person yourself too.

Relationships

Relationships will be loving and fulfilling this month. You will find joy in the company of family and friends. There may be a child birth in your family. A young person around you may need your guidance in matters of love. Your intuitions are telling you to stay cautious of certain person(s). Listen to that, heed to the advice of your instincts and act accordingly.

Health

Health will be good. If you have been struggling with an illness, recovery might be faster this month as you find a way ahead with the right doctor or course of treatment. Menopausal changes might create some problems for you. Also those going through rehab or considering it, it will bring good changes into your life although it may be a tough journey ahead. But it is something that you are completely capable of undertaking.

Spirituality

Do not run away from the call of the spirit. You have been guided to make some changes in your life but the longer you avoid, the more difficult the journey gets. Learn to go with the flow. Make the journey easier. Your intuitive capabilities support you immensely in this regard.

March

Work

You are brimming with new ideas at work. But you may find it difficult to implement them this month as a lot of changes are going on at the workplace. You may experience some chaos or uncertainty at the workplace or with your business. It is important right now to keep yourself steady and stay focussed. You may have to be flexible with your plans as there is likely to be some unpredictability about the environment in which you operate.

Finances

Financially this month may prove to be a tad bit challenging. Unexpected expenses may throw your budget off course. You may also come across certain seemingly attractive investment opportunities. It is important to see through the good and bad in all of it to make a better decision. Money may flow in from an unexpected source at the last minute. Believe in having abundance. Things will get better soon.

Love

A proposal may come your way from someone that you have been longing waiting for. However cards advise caution at this point because not everything may be as you had imagined. People are not just how we see them, they have many different facets to them that become visible in different circumstances. Do not take a rest decision. If your gut says something is not quite right or if you are doubtful, take your time before all information about the person is revealed up close.

Relationships

Good times with friends and family are on the cards. An addition to the family is indicated. You may be playing the role of a mentor to a young adult in the family. Friends will be supportive and celebrations with friends will provide an opportunity for letting off the steam from work. Visitors may keep you busy this month so you may need to plan ahead your schedule accordingly.

Health

Health will be average with occasional colds and flu due to a lowered immune state. Do not shy away from taking care of your health by doing little things everyday to maintain and improve immunity and stamina levels. Having better control over your food and lifestyle may come easier this month.

Spirituality

Remember to have compassion for yourself just as much as you tend to have for others. You can get too hard on yourself at times especially when pursuing goals in life. Your most important parts of life are in the present. Live in the now as well. Cancerians are soft and gentle beings but can be obsessive as well. Watch your obsessiveness regarding people or goals this month.

April

Work

New avenues and opportunities for work seem to be opening up this month for you. As you prepare yourself for the new roles and jobs, you also need to prepare for the fast pace of work that won't give you an opportunity to think. Offers from overseas for a job or a business opportunity will be tempting and it is likely to align with your skill set. Stay open to learning on the job as well. Keep learning otherwise your skills will be outdated in this fast changing world.

Finances

Finances will be good this month but you also need to prepare for the future expected needs. Do not let any expenditure catch you off-guard. You may tend to worry this month about payments that are due as they may get delayed uncomfortably. Any investment in the stock market or risky instruments this month needs to be watched carefully as the changes are likely to be so quick that you may miss the opportune window.

Love

Success in matters of love is on the cards. If you have been looking for love, this might just be your lucky month. For those in relationships, this is likely to be a good time to talk about the future. There may be some hurdles especially related to time, but nothing that cannot be sorted out with some effort. Ensure your expectations of each other are communicated openly and agreed upon before taking any further steps. In matters of marriage, don't just look for love, look for compatibility as well.

Relationships

A mother figure in your life will play an important role in your life at this time. You may get to spend some quality time with her. It may be that she tends to frustrate or irritate you at times, but learn to strike a balance and know what to talk about. It will help you relate with her better. You may feel conflicted about a family situation. Instead of making decisions based on the short term feelings, consider the long term impact.

Health

Health will be good overall. If you have been trying for a baby, this is the right time for it. New approaches to health and issues related, will be favourable and bear good results. Instead of worrying about a health concern, it is advisable to do something about it. Get a full health checkup done and consult a good doctor in case something persists.

Spirituality

As you work towards your goals, the universe supports you in every way possible. It is likely that you may have been resisting some change in your life or perhaps some feelings within yourself. Let go of the resistance and allow those difficult feelings some expression too. Remember, the more you resist, the more it persists. Allow, let go and find your freedom to move ahead.

May

Work

Work will be good. You will be productive and efficient this month. You are likely to meet your targets and perhaps even outperform. Work environment will be pleasant and supportive. An opportunity that you have been waiting for is likely to come to you this month. A new offer for a job or a business opportunity will be exactly something you have been preparing yourself for. Don't second guess yourself. You are ready and you can do it.

Finances

Finances will be good this month, yet there may be some uncertainty about receiving your dues. A promotion is on the cards. You will benefit from consulting work this month. Share your wisdom along with your resources with those who you mentor and guide. It will come back to you manifold. A risky investment is likely to give good returns. But don't make this into a habit. This will be a good time to start an investment plan for retirement or future needs.

Love

If you have been meaning to ask someone out but haven't gathered the courage yet, this is the time to do it. Don't overthink it, you have already dreamt of it for so long. Be yourself, don't try to be someone else in your relationships, especially the most intimate ones. Balance your personal relationships with your professional life, this warning comes in as you are likely to prioritise your relationship over a very good professional opportunity. Know your priorities.

Relationships

Someone among your friends or family is trying to play dirty games or backstab you. Stay aware and trust your instincts. You are capable of spotting a scheme from afar, don't let your emotions get the better of you in such cases. There are people genuinely willing to help you. Don't shut them off. Remember to keep your well-wishers close, don't punish them for someone who ends up disappointing you.

Health

Health will be good this month. Though you may experience elevated stress levels. This might upset your blood pressure or sugar levels. So keep a close eye on that. If you are planning to start a new diet or health regimen, this is a good time to do that. However, don't just keep planning. Get started with it. Make it a part of your everyday life so it doesn't feel like an extra effort.

Spirituality

A family situation requires healing and love. If you have been struggling with it, remember, strife is a result of some form of fear or anger. The answer or solution to that is love. It doesn't mean you love your enemies even when they can bite you. But you can send loving energies to them. When you send harsh energies to them, they come back to you manifold. So consider sending love energetically for a change.

June

Work

You will take charge of situations at the workplace this month. You may even be assigned a leadership or management role to take care of certain matters at work. Your skill with handling people will come in handy this month as you may experience some unpleasantness and conflicts in the work environment. A need to deal delicately with clients is important otherwise the deal might go sour or not materialise at all.

Finances

Financially this will be a good month. You will feel abundant, may even donate to a cause and be able to help someone in the family. Don't try to hold on to anything for fear of lack. A major premium payment or a loan might get paid off this month which will be a cause of celebration. Count your blessings and remember to invest your energies in growing the money through investing.

Love

This may not be the best month regarding matters of love. You may experience disappointment, rejection or heartbreak. Something that you had been putting off for some time or even avoiding it will need to be dealt with this month. But the good aspect is that you will be able to deal with all of this with grace and learn from your experiences as well. Look at the silver lining always no matter how dark the clouds.

Relationships

You sometimes end up taking more responsibility for everyone around you than what is needed. Situations this month might remind you that the world is not your responsibility and that you need to let others take their responsibility as well. Friends and family will seek out your help this month. It is best to discern who really needs to be helped and who needs to just be motivated to help themselves.

Health

Health will be good. A recurring illness might bother you this month but it is also a reminder to do something permanent about it rather than treating the symptom. An emotional cleanse and detox will be good for health this month as you may indulge in excesses this month burdening your system.

Spirituality

Every time we face challenges, we are propelled deeper into seeking answers within. It is a trigger for our growth if only one can recognise it. This month you may experience many such triggers, use them instead of delving into self pity. Use them to grow within, go deeper into your spiritual practices and connect with yourself. Practice compassion for yourself.

July

Work

This month you may feel a bit low on energy or motivation to complete your tasks. There is likely to be some confusion and doubts about your present job and hence you may be procrastinating taking action. It is best to talk to someone, perhaps a friend, to help to make sense of your doubts and feelings. Pending work will demand your attention and you may have to do some overtime to finish the tasks at hand.

Finances

Financially this may be a tough month as you struggle to meet the expenses. A loan you had been expecting may not come through easily or in the desired amount, creating dissatisfaction and some disappointment. You may feel worried about meeting the needs financially but worry is not going to help. This is time to take charge and think through things clearly. Your ideas are worthwhile. You just need to remove the distractions and focus on implementing the ideas.

Love

Memory from a breakup from the past or an ex-lover's thoughts might keep you occupied and make you feel uncomfortable. Doubting your decisions about that is not going to help in any way. You may have conflicting feelings about people you are seeing presently. You may have to look at the new people from a fresh perspective instead of comparing them to someone from your past.

Relationships

Relationships can be a source of comfort this month. However, you may have to cut ties or take a break from certain people in your life, especially if they have been bothering you. Choose to be with people who uplift you instead of being with those who make you feel bad about yourself. You don't have to give the benefit of doubt to everyone. Trust your instincts in this matter. A close friend is willing to support you and hear you out. Reach out for help.

Health

Health will be average. You may experience low energy levels and a general feeling of lethargy and inertia. You may also experience sleeplessness or incessant looping thoughts. An emotional drain or overwhelm could be the most likely cause for this. Watch who you meet or interact with and clear your energies often. Taking salt water baths this month will be very healing.

Spirituality

It is important for you to extend the compassion you have for others to yourself as well. You are allowed to feel low and also to make mistakes. Learn from your mistakes instead of calming yourself for making them. Dedicate yourself to learning a new course or attending a workshop related to emotional wellbeing this month.

August

Work

This month will be a busy time at work as you are dedicated to meeting the deadlines at work place. You are likely to handle more than one task at hand and that may cause elevated stress levels. Try to distribute your workload. Perhaps you have taken on more than you can chew. With so much on your plate right now, do not take on any added commitments as you may not be able to fulfil them. Worrying about work and deadlines is only going to make things more difficult. Stay calm and focus on one thing at a time.

Finances

Finances will be good this month. You are likely to receive opportunities from abroad that will add to your income sources in the coming months. You will take on the task of helping those around you financially as well. But this can backfire as those you may end up losing money, resources as well as certain people who you considered friends or close. Keep your tendency to help everyone in check and only help those who really need it.

Love

You may end up disappointing someone or being disappointed with them. Love matters will be at the back burner as you tend to focus on your work and work related matters this month. This attitude may even be a distraction from a heartbreak that you have recently endured. If that is so, it won't help for long. You will need to address the emotions and feelings soon enough if you really wish to move on.

Relationships

You may experience some rifts in your relationships this month as you try to sort out your priorities. This is a month when you will be reminded that those who matter would not mind you taking some time out for yourself and your work. And those who mind are certainly people who you don't want in your life anymore. Let go of people who don't uplift you. This is likely to be a month of facing such situations.

Health

Health will be fine. Your efforts are giving results and this is a confirmation to keep going on. You may need to consult experts in matters of health. At the same time you also need to listen to your body and follow its intelligence. If you have been planning for a baby and working towards it, you may see success in that direction this month.

Spirituality

Some of the biggest challenges in our life stem from a lack of self acceptance. This month brings you lessons and experiences that will make you look at this aspect of yourself and work on it. If you make decisions from a place of accepting yourself unconditionally, most decisions will seem easy and not tough. This is one piece of the missing puzzle for you that will make a huge difference in your life.

September

Work

Work will be good and will keep you busy this month. Promotion to a managerial or a leadership role is on the cards. You will be busy working on creating foundational aspects of your business or a project or venture. Creating work-life balance this month will be difficult but necessary as you are to preserve your focus and clarity of mind. Remember to take breaks and not to stress yourself too much about anything. Take all that comes in your stride.

Finances

Finances will be good. A partnership venture may be offered to you which will bring in much abundance. Remember to make your financial decisions wisely and don't feel out counsel or discuss it with many people. You are equipped enough to make your decisions. Trust yourself. You may want to learn something related to finances or your field of work in order to create a better position for yourself.

Love

You are likely to wear your heart on your sleeve this month. Love offers and proposals will be plenty. You may even want to propose to the one whom you have your heart set on. However in all these matters, do seek advice before jumping the gun. Your heart may at times lead you astray. It is important to stay grounded and also think through the practical matters of life before getting into a relationship with a certain individual.

Relationships

Certain relationships are not as bad as you may be thinking. This is the time to give benefit of doubt to those around you and don't take things personally. There may be periods of time this month when you feel lonely or you have no one to share your thoughts with. It is better to keep to yourself rather than share your mind and heart with someone who may not be your well wisher. There may be stillness in family matters. But stillness does not mean conflict. Make peace with it.

Health

Health will be average, though you may experience occasional headaches or sprains in the body. Whenever you feel physically low, explore what is going on emotionally within you. Chances are it is directly correlated. Don't try to push yourself too hard just to prove yourself to someone. Sticking to your routine will be of utmost importance this month.

Spirituality

You may find yourself standing at fork roads wondering which path is the best. Remember to choose the one which feels right. It may not be the easy one. You will be tempted to give in to your emotional cravings this month but it is not in abstinence but self acceptance that you will find peace and growth. Be kind to yourself and don't give in to the temptation of short term pleasures as it could wreak havoc with your life.

October

Work

Work will be good. You will find yourself in a position of consolidating your gains and all that you have created this month. You are ready to move on, either to a new job, new project or a new place of work. However, your attachment to the present place and to its environment which has become sort of a comfort zone is making it hard to make the decision. But you will have to choose sooner than later. Don't get attached to your work but focus on your growth.

Finances

Finances are good this month. Yet you will feel as if it's not enough. It's your feeling of lack, stemming from past experiences, that will not let you enjoy the goodness in the present moment. Your investments are doing good and you may even want to consider new investment schemes or avenues for future growth. There is no need to worry about money this month. Too much thinking can cause paralysis of action. Stay aware.

Love

A new relationship or love can blossom, bringing much happiness and joy for you. Your carefree attitude makes you more attractive and brings interesting people into your life. People will want to be part of your life and be in your presence as they find it very comforting. Don't stay stuck in past experiences. It is over. Don't let it hold you back from experiencing love.

Relationships

Relationships will be a source of comfort and love. Your caring attitude helps keep the family together and is a glue that binds friends. People appreciate you for this quality. This month will bring much joy as you get to spend some quality time with friends and family. Vacation may be planned and get-togethers will keep the energy high.

Health

Health will be good. However, you are likely to indulge in excesses this month which can cause some problems with digestion, acidity and metabolism. Keep up your active lifestyle and exercises as a part of your routine. If you are experiencing any changes in the body, activity and routine and consistency with it will take care of most issues. Pick one activity and do it consistently.

Spirituality

Spiritually you may feel as if this is the end of an era and the beginning of a new one. You have been through tough times and tough lessons. But it is of no use spending too much time ruminating about them. Take the lessons and move on. Experience joy, it is not something you find outside, it is something you feel inside. One of the strongest ways of experiencing joys is to actively seek joy in your everyday life.

November

Work

Work will keep you busy this month. However you may experience some disappointment at work. It could be regarding a teammate who did not support you in a way you expected or a work project that did not fare as well as you planned. But remember, it does not mean it was a failure. It still did good, just not how you expected. Keep yourself busy with doing constructive work, learn from your mistakes and move ahead.

Finances

Finances will be good. New sources of income will be welcome. You are likely to be able to pay off a major chunk of any loans that you had. However the little unexpected expenses might trouble you this month as they represent roadblocks to your mental peace. Instead of looking at them as hurdles, perhaps look at them as blessings that you have a good life, hence the bills and the ability to pay them. Don't invest in risky short term ventures this month.

Love

There will be a certain maturity in your love relationship this month. As the dynamics change, you will need to recognise the need for you to change how you approach relationships and your role in them. You don't always have to be the one who provides or is useful, a relationship can be based on mutual sharing. It is time for you to address your codependency and heal it and stop enabling others through that.

Relationships

Your role as a giver and mentor will continue in the family environment. A young one around you will need your guidance and support at this time. Do not indulge in unnecessary conflicts or arguments with friends and family. If you need to put a point across, do so assertively and politely. Spend some time enjoying with family in activities that are fun for everyone.

Health

Health will need some attention this month. You may be tempted to do too much for your body and mind, but it is not recommended. You will need to balance work-outs with rest. Energy levels will be decent. Do not get influenced by new fads, instead listen to your body intelligence and work with it.

Spirituality

This month is likely to be spent on doing more inner work than being active externally. You may be urged to look at life and situations in a very different manner that is likely to change your whole outlook towards life and existence. Call for help from your guides, mentors or invite a guru in your life to help you navigate these changes.

December

Work

Work may be slow this month but your energy and drive will be high. This can cause certain conflicts within you and consequently in your work environment. Certain projects or business opportunities that you have been waiting for may not follow the timelines causing more anxiety for you. All they need is more work and perseverance. Don't give up so easily. Follow your instincts and do your bit.

Finances

Finances will be good. You will receive the resources that you have been waiting for. The loans are likely to be sanctioned providing you much relief and paving the way ahead for further work. This will be time to look at your existing investment and make any changes necessary to get the maximum returns. It is important to enjoy your abundance too. So spend some money on yourself too occasionally.

Love

Matters of love and heart may give you some anxiety or worries. But they will be unfounded because you can easily resolve any issues, if there are any. It could also be that your mind is making mountains out of molehills at the moment. So discuss with someone close, communicate and trust yourself to make the right decisions. If you are looking for love, instead of worrying about it, go out and meet some people. This is the time to take action.

Relationships

This month may be crucial regarding your relationships with family and friends. You will be required to stand firm and be assertive about your needs and respect yourself enough to make some tough decisions. Even if it means letting go of certain people. It may be that you may have to let go of certain expectations from those around you and accept them for who they are and embrace them with their eccentricities.

Health

Health will need attention this month. You cannot just ignore little signs and symptoms. Get yourself checked and deal with it. There is no point in avoiding it or expecting things to heal themselves. Don't stay indoors for very long, go out and meet and interact with people to maintain good mental health. It is time to make some major changes in your life, lifestyle and your perspective towards yourself and others. Seek help for physical and mental well-being.

Spirituality

Karma is just cause and effect. You cannot blame karma if something bad happens to you. Your actions and decisions are your karma. It is time to become aware of these subtle vibrations. Raise your vibrations through good karmas - positive actions and thoughts, prayers, affirmations, healing and acceptance.

Leo

July 23–August 22

Overview

2023 will be a busy year for you. That's one way to describe how Leos like to do something when they are passionate about an idea. You may literally feel like you are running in a race, sometimes even feel like the life you see is a blur because of the speed with which you will be moving.

You are likely to be involved in multiple projects and they won't be one at a time, but simultaneous. You will juggle with many ideas. One of the challenges however would be to keep the big picture in mind before charging ahead.

The challenges that 2023 is going to throw up will not be a piece of cake but also not so tough that you will have a hard time dealing with them. You are likely to learn lessons in humility and also fathom the extent of your strength.

Health might take a hit as you will be doing something contrary to your nature - thinking too much. Planning is not one of your strongest suits but executing is. But this is a blessing because you won't be ruminating all in your head but taking action on it. Your rashness at times could lead you into health problems like stress headaches, migraines and dehydration. Digestive disorders will keep troubling you and will require you to be watchful of your lifestyle and taking active care of your health.

On the personal front this year will bring about many changes in the dynamics of your relationships and in general how you handle your life. Unpredictability may provide a sense of lack of stability but will also provide the much needed variety you crave for. Many goals on the personal front will see the light of the day and be achieved. Marriage, children and spiritual development are all on the cards.

Professionally, life and work will keep you busy. Many new projects will be started but only those that provide satisfaction and money will be alive by the end of the year. You will be quick with making decisions and cutting your losses with your sharp insight. Some of you may even choose to do an apprenticeship under a master to learn the nuances of your work.

First half of the year will be about planting the seeds, doing the background work on many projects that you intend to do, applying for internships and receiving job offers that don't offer you much money but a lot of experience. Second half of the year will be the time when you begin to see the results of your hard work. Anything that you pursue with persistence this year will pay hefty dividends. Financially this seems to be a bountiful year. Socially you will be occupied. In the humdrum of this fast paced life, find some time, some quiet moments for yourself and your connection to the higher one.

January

Work

2023 starts with a bang as you land up with a long awaited opportunity in business or a job or more likely a position that you had been vying for some time. You are in a good place where you can choose your way ahead. Some of those choices may seem controversial or unexpected, but if it is your heart's calling, follow it. Any difficulties you have had at work will soon be a thing of the past.

Finances

Financially your position is likely to be strong, yet worries about money and liquidity can give you sleepless nights. Do not be tempted to look at short term gains in order to meet your requirements. Think long term or else you may end up with a losing bargain. This is the time to keep your money close and don't spend it all on showing your abundance to the world. You have been operating from a place of lack when it comes to money. It is time to switch into the abundance mindset.

Love

In matters of the heart, you are likely to let go of what you have at present because it doesn't resonate with who you are rather than compromise. Although it's an admirable quality, however, notice if you have been too stubborn over something and is it worth giving a relationship up in which you have invested. The dynamics in your relationship are changing but that doesn't mean the old relationship cannot withstand the shifts.

Relationships

Family and friends will be a source of comfort and love. There will be opportunities for get-togethers, meet ups and family gatherings. Do not stand on the fence, rather step in and enjoy yourself. You do not have to be the centre of attention to enjoy a gathering. Loved ones will support you. Marriage in the family will keep you busy. Acknowledge the love people shower on you rather than questioning their intentions always.

Health

Health will be good. Recoveries from any illnesses that may have been bothering you are on the cards. You will receive good care from quality professionals and doctors. Get in touch with your emotions too as it will open doors to healing and a healthy lifestyle. Your healing abilities will also be called upon to help others suffering from physical or emotional issues.

Spirituality

You may undertake a course or mentoring for a particular subject related to healing or energy work. It has been calling to you for some time now and this is the right phase to begin. Dedication to your study and practice is your service to mankind. Every time you feel doubtful about your abilities, shift your perspective to being of service to others.

February

Work

Your ideas regarding your work or business are good. But you also need to be practical about their implementation. This is a good time to brainstorm and look at new creative opportunities. This will be a good month for you to reach out to new clients or client base and connect with more people. You have the abilities to pull any project or work through but it will require steadiness and patience which may be missing this month. Don't get bored or disappointed so quickly. Persistence is the key.

Finances

A move is on the cards. Financially it may be difficult for you but you will have the required support and assistance to see it through. You may also end up investing in venture or financial schemes suggested by your close friends or family. Take a good look at it before going ahead with it. Expenditure will be on the rise. A partnership will be fruitful, perhaps a partnership in investing in a major real estate or venture. You are in the right headspace to make good decisions that will affect your life to come in the next few months.

Love

If you are looking for love, you will need to jump into it fully. A half hearted approach will not help. You need to heal from recent breakups or separation before moving on. Process the grief, loss or rejection before you invite someone else into your life. Rebound relationships don't always work. The past is behind you. This is a good time to look ahead instead of looking in the past. It will be difficult to make decisions this month in matters of the heart but deep down you know the truth and the right path.

Relationships

Relationships will be fulfilling and give you much joy and happiness. You will be able to spend some good and happy time with your loved ones and the extended family. A celebration in the family is on the cards. It will be a happy moment for everyone involved. A loved one may be moving out for studies or to pursue a life of their own. Support them with love, as this will be a new beginning of sorts for you too.

Health

Health will be good. Your recent efforts for your health will bear fruits as you come close to achieving your goals. You may tend to indulge yourself this month but you will also be kind and tough enough for yourself to watch your steps. There is no harm in celebrating a success with occasional indulgence. A family member will need your care and support.

Spirituality

This month will present its own set of challenges and lessons that will aid in your spiritual growth. You are working in the right direction and all your work will lead you to a better place mentally and emotionally. Follow the moon cycles and watch your body rhythms. They are your key to understanding your lifestyle.

March

Work

Work will be good and fulfilling. However you may find time to be a listing factor in trying to achieve all your dreams. Deadlines this month can hamper the quality of your work, so it is suggested to pay attention to time and keep procrastination at bay. If you are looking for a new job, this is a good time to make efforts in that direction. You will get good results soon. You may face criticism from your superiors, instead of taking it personally, use it constructively for your work.

Finances

You may tend to see some uncertainty regarding finances this month. Though there may not be a lack of it, yet it would be a cause for worry at times. Stay away from speculation and risky investments as it could prove wasteful. You will need to have a tighter rein on your money matters this month to make sure you don't end up spending in one of your lion king like impulses. Don't let too much thinking cloud your decisions.

Love

If you are looking forward to having something more committed with your partner, this is a good time to broach the subject with them. You also need to make sure you are ready for this step. If you are single and looking for love, you need to first understand what you really want. It is better to have clarity yourself than leaving someone else confused and hurt. Stay away from any dramas in your relationship.

Relationships

This month you may want some time for yourself to gather your scattered energies, recharge yourself for another bout of socialising adventures and to just find some peace of mind. Don't try to please everyone around you. It will only leave you and those around you feeling more hurt and annoyed. Sometimes you don't have to fight the obstacles, rather go around them. Not everything needs to be aced head on.

Health

Health will be average, yet worried about your health might give you sleepless nights. It is better to get yourself a check-up than worry about something that could be wrong. It is time to embrace an active lifestyle. You may want to take up sports as a means of fitness as well to let off some excess steam.

Spirituality

This is time for active work. Activities like meditation and the zen mode may not be the right fit for you at this moment. Choose to do more service and active work like being coached for yourself. It is also time to give your service to others in any way possible for you. If you feel stuck and stagnant, this is the time to ask yourself, "How can I be of service?"

April

Work

Work will keep you occupied this month. You may also want to use it as a means for escape from something difficult going on around you. You are likely to have good rapport with your peers and subordinates. You may even take on the role of mentoring some of them. Your dedication to your work is likely to get you noticed by the right people. A new job offer may soon land in your lap. Weigh the pros and cons diligently before taking it up.

Finances

Finances this month may seem unpredictable with expected spendings that come up at the most unlikely times. You may need to balance the energy at home unless you want to spend a lot on getting things fixed that get broken often. This is the time to guard your savings. Do not give in to the temptation of spending on something that you don't need at the present moment. Stay grounded and practice moderation.

Love

Your love life will be a source of pleasure and comfort. If you are looking for a partner, you are likely to meet one this month. There will be good chemistry and it is likely to have potential for the future. For the ones in a relationship, committed or not, this is time to take a closer look at your priorities and see if you are treating your better half in a good manner. Relationships need time and nurturing, are you giving yours enough?

Relationships

Relationships will need to be handled delicately this month as you may encounter some situations that may look too good to be true. They are likely to be traps but they might be difficult to avoid. However it does not mean you shut yourself out. Brace yourself and handle the devil with caution and care. There will also be some happy moments in the family. A get together with friends will give you much happiness and relief.

Health

Health will be average. If recovering from an illness, you will find good results this month. Don't get too confused about any action to take. Seek expert advice or may be a second opinion. Complete recovery is to be expected. Keep up with your health and fitness routines. Take care of your mental and emotional health as well.

Spirituality

Whatever ideas you have been thinking of or working towards, they are good. Work on them and you will find the way ahead. Don't plan too much into the future. Live in the moment, in the now. Angels are always there to assist you, you only need to ask. This is a good time to pursue any courses in spiritual fields. They will enrich you with wisdom and experience.

May

Work

This month you may see the momentum slowing down, even giving you a breather for a change. This is time to consolidate all that you have done so far, take stock of the situation, plan for the future and figure out how to execute it. You may feel the need to take a break from the fast pace and enjoy the fruits of your endeavours. You are likely to receive multiple offers or opportunities for the future, so much so that you find it difficult to decide. Take your time choosing and allow more information to pour in before making any decisions.

Finances

It may feel like a tough road ahead sometimes when it comes to finances. Managing your budget may pose a challenge this month. You may even look for certain new investments. Be cautious and prudent, setting money aside at this moment and tying it up in locked investment schemes. You may need to look for additional sources of income and work on building them up for the future. Be wary of giving out loans to friends as the money may not come back to you.

Love

Marriage is on the cards this month. You may be tempted to take action, do something but this is the time to allow things to flow. Stay balanced. Don't give in to impulsive decisions. Think them through, consult your elders or well-wishers, especially in the matters of the heart. Don't get into a relationship just because you feel lonely. Find the right reasons. Sometimes matters of the heart need to be thought through rather than just go with the feelings.

Relationships

You are likely to be on good terms with most people around you right now. A new friendship might enter your life bringing in a fresh perspective. You will need to guard your decisions and actions more carefully right now as there is a likelihood of others trying to influence your decisions and actions. It may not be entirely for your benefit. It is important for you to stay playful in your relationships and don't let seriousness dull the fun.

Health

Your health will be good overall, but you will need to be more careful with your health issues this month as they might trouble you occasionally. Don't experiment with new fad diets or health programs as they may do more damage than good. Follow your trusted process, do your work and stay persistent with it. Your efforts may not yield results immediately but the rewards will come for sure.

Spirituality

You are going through a period of intense changes and growth. This period can be confusing and exhausting. Often, the changes are happening on the inside. Give yourself enough compassion, kindness and rest to allow these changes to help you outgrow your older self. Invoke the healing energies of Archangel Raphael this month to help you move through this phase effortlessly.

June

Work

This month you will be working with both your masculine as well as feminine energies. It means you will be working relentlessly, with focus and yet in an effortless manner. This is a rare combination, but for Leos this can be possible. You have the ability to see through a lot of information for its benefits and uselessness. Your perseverance will help you complete your work in time and also gain praise from your peers and others who work with you. Overall a good month for you.

Finances

Even though you have been trying hard to have surplus funds at the end of the month, it somehow hasn't been happening. This month you may finally be able to figure out the leaks, plug them and find a new approach to handle your finances with prudence. There is no use being worried over things that are not always in your control. What you can do is not assume the grass to be greener on the other side, water your garden and tend to your situation. This month you may have developed a new perspective towards finances and money.

Love

Getting into a relationship is on the cards. Even if you are in a relationship, nurturing it is of prime importance. Take some time spending some quality moments with your partner, get to know them, share their joys and sorrows. Communicate clearly to resolve any misunderstandings. You may need to take some alone time too this month. But let your partner know about it clearly that it's not about them so they don't take it personally.

Relationships

You may enjoy your own company this month more than people's. It is ok to say no to their demands on your time and attention. You need to tend to yourself first, fill your cup before you can give to others. It is also ok to stand your ground when your friends or family are trying to pile on their stuff or demands on you or force you to do something. This month will test your strength in the face of your loved ones and standing up to them.

Health

Health will be good this month as you consistently make efforts towards improving it and keeping yourself in good shape. You may tend to indulge yourself in food and other substances this month. While it's ok to do so once in a while, don't make it a habit to just please or connect with someone. Weather may affect you adversely this month, stay hydrated and pay attention to the body.

Spirituality

This will be a month when you will be confronted with your shadows and limitations. While it is not a pleasant experience, this will be a good time to pay attention to it and heal it by embracing it. If it feels overwhelming, reach out to your mentor, coach or guide to help you take the journey of healing and make peace with the past instead of running away from it.

July

Work

Work this month may not be as you had expected. The pace might slow down which may cause frustration for you. There may be unexpected delays and hurdles in an otherwise smooth flow which can delay your deadlines and upset your schedules. Take this in your stride instead of getting worked up about it. Some flexibility and a sense of playfulness will help you ride through things. Work environment will be good. Use this time to connect with people and expand your network.

Finances

Financially things are beginning to look up. Money tied up in an investment or a loan given out is likely to find its way back to you. Stay open to miracles for manifesting abundance and inflows from unexpected sources. Even though money flow is opening up, you may find yourself still worrying about the lack of it. It is time to move from a lack to abundance mindset. Finances are likely to get better in the coming months.

Love

As love knocks on your door, make sure you are ready for it. A chance meeting with someone new could ignite passion and kindle a new romance. You will spend good quality time with your partner. Find activities that are mutually enjoyable and indulge in it. This will further strengthen the bond. If you need help or are unsure of something in your relationship, instead of worrying about it, say it out loud. Open and clear communication can help resolve most challenges.

Relationships

Your relationships this month with friends and family can be a challenging aspect to deal with. You may struggle with the past baggage that a certain person brings with them and are perhaps not ready to look beyond it. But don't let this hesitation send you on a guilt trip and then overcompensate for that by giving away your power and love. Stay balanced, it's ok to take some time to process the changes happening in the relationship. You deserve to take a fresh look and take your time doing it.

Health

Health is likely to be good this month. A moderate approach to any health program is better for you rather than pushing yourself to extremes and punishing yourself for it. Alternative approaches to healing and health will be beneficial for you. This is a good time to get your energy cleansed and chakras cleared for better health, focus and a peaceful mind. Be playful and don't take anything very seriously. Do the work and enjoy it as well. Health is not always gained by punishing yourself.

Spirituality

This is a good time to indulge in activities like meditation, energy healing and other spiritual practices. It will help you raise your vibrations from stress, fear and doubt to clarity, calmness and peace. It will not only help you focus better but also make you feel good about yourself and energetic. Invest in your emotional and mental health. Learn something new this month.

August

Work

Work will be good and any obstacles in completing your projects will clear away as you move ahead with confidence and focus. If you have been thinking of changing your career field or profile, this is a good time to work towards it. You have the right ideas, there is still more to do when it comes to implementing them. You may feel like taking a break and you deserve it too. But don't let it break your flow for long.

Finances

You may feel the burden of expenses this month as they file up unexpectedly. You will receive support for meeting your requirements from good sources and it will also help lift you out of problems or stuckness. Be open to receiving help from those around you. A loan that you had been waiting for is likely to be cleared up this month. Even though the expenses are increasing, the money also flows in almost miraculously. Stay grateful and choose abundance over worries.

Love

There is going to be a change in the dynamics of a love situation which can be unsettling for both you and your partner. However it is long due, so instead of avoiding it, face it with serenity as it will create something better for you in terms of a relationship. Something about your partner may come to light which could make you feel betrayed. But it will be your choice how to act and what to choose going ahead. Things are changing, it is not easy but essential.

Relationships

This month you may feel like there are two people inside you pulling you in opposite directions. On one hand, you will want to make decisions quickly and rather harshly. But the other part of you will want you to sleep over it, think and then act. This month will be a challenging act in many ways. You will also be busy with meeting and socialising different groups that could be taxing for your senses and body. Choose what's important for you and act accordingly.

Health

A seasonal health issue might prove to be more stubborn than you had imagined. It may take some time to be healed completely. Give yourself the healing time and space. This is also a good time to plant seeds for new habits related to health. You will be inspired to modify your lifestyle and food habits that will serve you well eventually. Don't worry too much, connect with nature to calm yourself and your mind.

Spirituality

You are in manifestor mode right now. Anything you say or ask for can manifest quickly and easily. Allow yourself to use this power to create goodness and health instead of worrying about situations. You have done your inner work and this is a result of your efforts. Keep up with them and practice gratitude for whatever you have manifested and are in the process of manifesting.

September

Work

This month you are likely to be overburdened with work and responsibilities. Work life balance may go for a toss. You will be busy with teamwork and working with people will be enjoyable as well as stimulating for you. Your work will produce the results as per your expectations. Superiors and clients are likely to be happy with your work and work ethics. This is the time to pick up projects that are viable and financially profitable rather than those that are easy but don't have good financial viability.

Finances

Finances will be average. They are getting better but need more time and patience from your end. You are doing what you can, you have made certain decisions. Right now there is nothing more that you can do except for waiting and expecting the best to happen. Don't worry too much about things not happening actively. There are times of activity and then there are times of rest. Respect the rhythms of life. A friend or an organisation with whom you have good ties will be forthcoming with the money and resources that you need at the present.

Love

Love life will be full of sparks, passion and zest. There is likely to be some minor tussle with your partner but some conflicts are expected and should be looked forward to. A relationship without any conflicts is most likely a dead one. Take it in your stride and consider it as the spice in your relationship. If you are looking for love, this is a good time as you are very likely to meet someone new who will help you look at life from a completely different perspective.

Relationships

This month it seems like the worst is over and is well behind you. Plenty of changes in your relationships can make you feel as if you are in a hurricane and it will feel difficult to find your feet again. Take your time, don't let this overwhelm you. Rest and taking a break from certain people and relationships is perhaps the best approach right now. These experiences also make you wiser when it comes to interacting with people and choosing friends.

Health

Health will be average. You have seen better days and this month will certainly seem to bring up some stuff and issues that can trouble you off and on. But the good news is that whatever is troubling you is most likely in its final stages before healing. The body takes time to heal the memory of the illness. Seek out a healer to help you release the cellular memory of the health issues and let healing take place energetically as well.

Spirituality

When all seems lost, that is when we need to look at all that we have still and all that we have gained from the experience. Focus on optimistic thoughts, keep doing your work consistently and pay attention to how you feel in your body. It is your compass to navigate the emotional map of your life.

October

Work

Work pace will be slow but steady. Some old projects are coming to a completion and give you the expected returns and rewards. You may experience some delays or hurdles at work or the orders from clients. Don't worry too much, it is just a delay not a denial. You may want to take a little break to gather your energies and refresh your mind this month. It is important to sometimes step back to have a look at the bigger picture before moving ahead.

Finances

You may see a change in the pace of inflow of money. Finances will not be a problem yet you may feel the stress associated with it mostly because of the many changes happening. This is not the time to accrue unnecessary expenditure. Guard your money, nurture your savings and have gratitude for all the goodness that universe has showered over you. A happy expense in the family is on the cards this month.

Love

If casual relationships are your thing, this is going to be a successful month for that. If you are looking for something steady, then the cards suggest you to wait and seek out the right person. You don't have to settle just because you feel lonely. If you are in a steady relationship or marriage, you may experience moments of worries about your interpersonal dynamics. Suggestion is not to worry but focus on having clear communication.

Relationships

You are likely to meet new people this month who have the potential to be good friends in future. Keep your hopes up. Family environment will be pleasant. There is likely to be some activity and travel with family this month. Listen to your heart and instincts when it comes to dealing with people. Your intuition will guide you in the best possible manner. Go out more often, don't stay at home to keep your energies moving.

Health

Health will be average. Some issues need care. Don't hesitate to seek support from people around you and from experts. Your ideas related to health are good, follow them with consistency. Focus on one path instead of trying to follow different things from different methods as it will only create more confusion for the body. Follow moderate approach in workout and lifestyle changes.

Spirituality

This is a time to preserve your energies. Stay focussed and do not scatter your energies unnecessarily. Choose the dramas and battles. You don't have to fight or participate in everything around you. Choosing is what brings wisdom and growth. Connect to your higher self and your spiritual guides for guidance. Meditation will really help this month in managing your stress levels and helping you with calmness.

November

Work

This month will bring in fresh opportunities and work. Job offers will be available if you are looking for a change. It is going to be a creative time and especially fruitful for those in creative professions. If you have been planning for expansion of business or branching out into new territories and products, this is a good time to take this ahead. You would not have to look back this month either in regret or in disappointment.

Finances

Financially this month may feel like a roller coaster ride as you are likely to see both highs and lows. New avenues for income and opportunities are opening up. Along with it uncertainty and doubts will also creep up causing you to think twice before moving ahead with a decision. There will be moments of celebration as you spend on some assets as well as dreams that you have had. Don't go too much into debt this month as it could create problems in future.

Love

This month you seem to be sitting on the fence and are hesitant about jumping into the pool of love. Matters of heart can be confusing but you won't be able to resolve them just by thinking or dreading them. You are likely to receive offers and proposals, some of them are likely to be very good as well. Don't reject them because of unrealistic expectations or fears that come from how things turned out in the past. Heal your heart, open it and move on.

Relationships

Relationships are going to be a mixed bag this month. You will experience happy moments with people you love and will be able to spend joyful times with them. You are also likely to experience disappointment and betrayal in one of your close relationships. This will be a good time to introspect on whether you have been burdening someone with your expectations instead of accepting them as they are.

Health

Health will not be satisfactory and will need care and attention this month. You seem to have been burdening yourself too much with stress and unnecessary worries. It is now beginning to affect your health. There is a need to detox yourself, put yourself in a routine and follow a healthy lifestyle. A retreat or a residential health program can benefit you immensely at this time. Be open to taking guidance from an expert in this matter.

Spirituality

Leos are used to being alone and working and solving problems on their own. But it is not always the best approach. Open your heart chakra and work with others as a team. It takes courage to be vulnerable. But only when you can let your guards down, can you begin to heal the wounds inside. Take help, work with a peer or a mentor and face shortcomings with grace and courage.

December

Work

Work will be excellent as you succeed in your goals and reap the rewards of your hard work. This month you may be in the process of finalising plans for growth and expansion, take on new projects or ventures and get ready for more responsibilities and leadership positions. Raise in stature and power is on the cards. You will establish yourself as an authority in your field of work. The environment and the people around you including your peers and superiors will support you and help you climb the ladder.

Finances

Though there is no real need for worry, yet you tend to get stressed over little things when it comes to situations or money going out of your control. Impulsive decisions could throw your financial plans in jeopardy, a little care is advisable. This is a good time to plant new seeds of investments and look for beneficial opportunities for financial growth and abundance. Don't spend your time and resources trying to prove yourself. Trust your strengths and blessings.

Love

There may be some communication problems in your relationship that will need your attention. You will need to invest time and energy into communicating clearly and lovingly with your partner otherwise there may be some serious misunderstandings. Make sure your heart is in the right place and your intent is pure when approaching someone for a relationship. New relationships will take time to grow. All they require is some nurturing.

Relationships

You may be torn this month between spending time with friends and family. Your family needs your attention right now as someone close to you needs your support and guidance. A young one in the family is ready to step into adulthood, support them with confidence. Do not stop them because you fear for them. You may experience some burn out this month from too much social interaction. Give yourself enough time and space alone for healing.

Health

Health is on the mend as you work diligently towards good health. Your cardiovascular health will need care and attention. Recovery from an illness is very near but it is going to be troublesome before it ends. A new way of approaching health and body will be helpful. Focus on emotional and mental health this week to cope with the stress of all that has happened in the year. If you have been ignoring your body, a health issue might bring your attention back to yourself.

Spirituality

As the year ends, it is time to take stock of your spiritual journey and see how far ahead you have come. This is a good time to revive your healing skills and send some healing energy to yourself and the earth. Spiritual experiences are likely to happen this month. Don't try to find too much meaning into it, rather accept it for what it is and keep going with your meditation and spiritual practices.

CHAPTER SEVEN

Virgo

August 23–September 22

Overview

2023 is a year of endings and new beginnings for you. This year brings in hope and optimism as you shed the old and embrace the new. It will come with its own set of challenges but no challenge is insurmountable for the persistent Virgo. This year will call upon your organisational and planning skills to help you wade through overload of work and responsibilities. But you will need to remind yourself of playfulness and adopt that attitude as you can tend to be quite serious when it comes to achieving goals.

New beginnings this year will keep you on your toes as you pursue higher studies to further your career. It might get a bit challenging to balance the home and work so remember to delegate and ask for help. There will be an abundance of feminine energy this year which will help you multitask with ease.

Your foresight is your strength in 2023. Use it to plan your year and months well ahead in advance as you would not want to be caught off guard with any new developments. There is an emphasis on your continuous growth and education to keep up to date with the new developments in your field. You will have the energy and aptitude to go through it.

In personal life, there is a lot to look forward to. It is time to start looking for people in your life who match your vibration and understand your worldview. You will also receive many opportunities for this as well. Professionally, this seems to be a year of success as you bask in the rewards of your efforts and persistence. You will be able to consolidate your position and it will be financially rewarding for you.

First half of the year is about hope and expecting the best. You may not have clarity and doubts may pull you back at certain crucial moments. But remember the star of hope as it guides you towards your success and purpose. Keep connecting to your higher purpose to find a way ahead. The second half of the year will bring in the results of your hard work and also bring a lot of attention along with it. Do not shy away from it. Use it to lead and guide others as well.

January

Work

Work will keep you busy this month. You may even feel overburdened as you take on more than you can handle. This will be a time to learn to delegate and focus on what's important. You may plan to hire new employees this month. Make sure your decisions are based on how much value they can provide you. You are likely to receive many opportunities and ideas. But not all of them are likely to be good. Pick and choose wisely.

Finances

You are well taken care of financially, yet your need to have it all sorted and clear can cause worry and anxiety at times. Your financial ideas are good and have merit, but their execution may be a challenge. This is a time to think through clearly each and every step you need to take to achieve your goals but at the same time you will also need to surrender and trust that all that you plan will be carried out in the best possible manner.

Love

This month you need to be careful in matters of love as you may attract and be charmed by those who need to take advantage of you. Seek out advice and counsel from your well-wishers before making any decision. Be optimistic as you don't have to settle for what comes your way. For those in a relationship, this is a good time to reignite the spark in your connection. Spend quality time with your loved one, take small breaks from work and life to rekindle your romance.

Relationships

Even though you approach relationships from a place of purity and innocence, yet a part of you always knows what's right for you and what's not. It is time to listen to that part more acutely as it is guiding you towards people who are good for your mental and emotional wellbeing and warning you from bringing the toxic ones into your life. A celebration in the family is on the cards. You are likely to spend joyous time with friends and family.

Health

If you have been ignoring a health issue, it will knock on your front door with persistence until you pay attention to it. Do not ignore any minor symptoms and get them checked out. Your ideas for health are good, it is time to put them into action and follow it with consistency. Worry about health is only going to make it worse. Pay attention to your emotional and mental health. Seek out help if necessary, but don't ignore it.

Spirituality

It is time to be honest with yourself. If you have been dealing with decisions and feeling stuck or wanting to maintain the status quo, perhaps you are not being honest about it with yourself. Look into your heart and ask what it is that it desires. Then act upon it. The longer you delay, the more difficult it gets to deal with it. When in doubt, ask yourself, "Does this bring me joy?"

February

Work

This month you may be torn between wanting to take a break and wanting to finish your pending work. A balance between the two is what is needed. You will be focussed on your projects at hand. There may not be much networking and interaction this month so the new opportunities may not open up so easily. But this is just a phase. Don't be too possessive about your wisdom, share your skills with your colleagues too.

Finances

Though you will be in an overall good place financially, yet there is likely to be some struggle around it. Don't try too hard and don't be worried about competition. Cards suggest you make peace with what you have instead of comparing it with others. a moderate approach in investing is advised. Stay away from risky investments especially those that seem to promise very high returns. Contentment with what you have will bring in more of it.

Love

Matters of love may cause some disappointment this month. If you have had a breakup, try to move on instead of holding on to what was good in that relationship. A new love beckons. Be willing to look for love and you will find it. For those in a steady relationship, your connection may seem to be fraught with some difficulties this month as there may be some ego clashes. Set aside your egos and focus on what is your priority. Communicate with love and seek to understand your partner's perspective as well.

Relationships

Friends will be a source of joy this month. You will spend good time with friends and family who you consider to be friends. Social gatherings and get-togethers are on the cards. A close loved one may cause disappointment and heartbreak. It is better to forgive and move on than harbour resentment in your heart as it only causes harm to you and no one else. This is a month to connect with yourself and the children around you as they remind you of your own inner child.

Health

Health will be good. Your consistent and persistent efforts will give you good rewards in terms of improving health, emotional stability and a sense of happiness. This month, focus on physical activity and workouts as they will be extremely beneficial for you. Seek to hire a trainer for added benefit.

Spirituality

You may go through some moments during this month when it may feel like the world is falling apart. These will be like those minor earthquakes that shake your foundations and force you to develop a new perspective for life and people. This will also be a reminder to not be a doormat, but be assertive of your needs and the right people will stay back. The wrong people will leave your life for good.

March

Work

This month the work will be slow. There are likely to be delays and overtime may be needed to complete your projects by deadline. Your hard-work and dedication will get you recognition from your team members and superiors. Team work will be of prime importance this month and you may have to set your differences aside to work as a team efficiently.

Finances

Financially this may be a difficult month. Payments might get delayed or stuck. This will also be a new development in the way of managing finances and a new perspective. An old source of income may become redundant and something new will develop soon. Your needs will be taken care of. Stay optimistic and positive.

Love

Matters of love may take a backseat as you get busy with work. Focus will be more on your personal growth this month. You may find it difficult to connect with new people this month. Take your time in making decisions about the matters of the heart. In your relationship with your partner, make an effort to communicate clearly about your personal changes and need time and space so that it doesn't not create any misunderstandings and strains.

Relationships

Relationships will be a source of comfort and happiness this month. You will find more personal space and support from your loved ones. You are ready to guide and mentor a young one around you. A celebration in the family may keep you busy as well. Marriage and child birth is on the cards.

Health

Health is likely to be good this month. Rigorous physical activity will be helpful in keeping your fitness levels up and keeping your thoughts in check, helping you stay calm and stress free. Take adequate rest to keep your energy level balanced. This may be a good time to start with a new health program with the help of an expert.

Spirituality

Relaxing is as important a part of human existence as is activity. This month take your time to relax without guilt, daydream sometimes as that is when the creative juices flow. Pay attention to your dreams as well. Dream work and dream journaling will be helpful in helping you connect to your inner self, your fears and desires.

April

Work

Work may be slow this month. New projects or job offers are likely to come your way. If this is something that you have been trying for some time, it is a good time to make use of these opportunities. A new partnership offer will be enticing for you and can become fruitful. You may struggle with low confidence as your self doubts may cause you to question your own competence and ability. Move past this doubt as it is just in your mind. Look at the evidence of all the good work that you have done.

Finances

Finances may cause you some worries this month as the money is likely to get stuck or delayed. This is not the time to have a proactive approach towards money and financing. You may have to be watchful about your expenditure as it may rise unexpectedly and throw your budget off course. But the good news is that financial worries will soon be a thing of the past. You are moving towards better times financially.

Love

In matters of love, your time and attention will be needed. A relationship that has been having problems and has run its course is likely to come to an end. You are emotionally ready to deal with the consequences of this. It is time to do some inner work related to your relationships this month as it will heal the wounds from the past and open doors for better and healthier relationships in the future.

Relationships

If you have been struggling to connect with people you love, it is time to put your insecurities aside and take the first step. Think from your heart and don't let your need for attention make you play any mind games here. Go out and enjoy with friends, connect with people in the family or outside and get in touch with your feelings. Express them, communicate them clearly to your loved ones, they deserve to know that you love them.

Health

Health needs time and attention this month. You may have been avoiding certain health issues and it is time to stop doing that and do something about it actively. Get your annual checkups, consult your doctor or healer, sign up for a health program. Take active steps to go out of our comfort zone, step out in the sun more often and have patience and persistence for whatever health goal you are working towards.

Spirituality

Get in the habit of listening to your heart more often. Your heart is an organ with intelligence of its own, and it's scientifically been proven now. You have been working from a sense of duty or righteousness, now is the time to start doing it from the heart. Take it easy, assert your needs, let people know what you think. Allow those who resonate with you to stay in your life and those who don't to leave.

May

Work

Work will be slow but satisfactory. New ways of working or new paradigms are likely to come in which will alter how you approach your work. This is a good phase as it will give you the required time and space to switch gears before moving ahead full steam. There may be some procedural delays but it will be for the best. New creative ventures will bring in more rewards. For those in the creative field of work, this is a good month.

Finances

If you have been working towards increasing your income, then you will need to leave your insecurities and doubts behind, work on your imposter syndrome and charge ahead with the tools you already have with you. Be open to reaching out to more people and becoming visible. This is a good time to change your gears and switch into the abundance mode. Finances are not the problem, it is how you perceive yourself with money that is the issue.

Love

This is a time of endings and new beginnings in matters of love. But there is likely to be a lot more action in this area of your life compared to the previous month. As you find closure and make peace with the past, new proposals come your way. These are likely to be very good and ones you should consider seriously before rejecting them. If you have been seeking reconciliation then this is a good time to work towards it.

Relationships

Relationships may be a challenge this month as you struggle to make sense of people's intentions. There may be some conflict in the family with your loved ones which could leave you disappointed and heartbroken. There are two ways you can handle this, either move away, create distance until the feelings settle or choose your battles wisely and don't engage in any unnecessary and avoidable arguments.

Health

Health is on the mend and getting better each day. However you may still be disappointed as your health program or routine is not giving results as quickly as you had expected. Go easy on yourself and celebrate the progress no matter how little. It may also be time to tweak your health routine and lifestyle to suit your needs better. Consistency and patience are the keys right now. Build your immunity and work towards dealing with any mineral or vitamin deficiencies.

Spirituality

Sometimes the universe is not seemingly doing anything because it is waiting for us to decide on a goal. So the best approach would be to decide a goal, and start working towards it. Meditation and other spiritual practices will help build your internal resources for manifestation and the required calmness for it. You may eventually choose to work for yourself and this is the right time to build your skills set for that.

June

Work

This month new opportunities will open up at the workplace into a new position or profile. However there may also be delays and the process can be painstakingly slow. Don't let this discourage you. Don't lose your patience either. New business could come into your hands but it may not be as fruitful as you had earlier imagined it to be. The work environment will be overall positive and uplifting. Keep taking occasional breaks to keep stress levels low.

Finances

Financially this is likely to be a positive month. Money will flow slowly but steadily. You will be able to receive help from all quarters. Pending loans will soon be cleared. Any fresh loans that you had applied for are likely to be sanctioned. Family inheritance matters may take your time but the results are likely to be positive in your favour. This month, keep a check on your spendings and focus on building a new investment portfolio.

Love

This is a good month in matters of love. If you are in a steady relationship, you will find time and a renewed connection with your partner that will bring much joy. If planning for a child, this is a good time. If you are looking for love, you will meet interesting people. They could be potential matches but the suggestion is not to settle. Be hopeful and keep looking for the right person will soon enter your life. Stay open to happy experiences.

Relationships

Relationships may demand time and attention as there are matters which need to be dealt with. You will need patience and steadiness to sort things out. You may experience anxiety and be worried about matters that are not in your hand and some of them may not be true as well. Situation is not as bad as you could be imagining. It is being coloured by your experiences from the past. You need to look at it from a fresh perspective and you will find that it's not something that cannot be dealt with.

Health

Health will be better this month. As you recover from a chronic illness, you will find new and alternative healing methods to heal yourself and sustain good health. Follow your intuition. You will find the right healer/doctor. Gut issues may trouble you this month along with some swelling and bloating problems. Focus on a healthy diet with more fibre and bitterness.

Spirituality

Your sense of trust and understanding comes from years of closely observing people and situations. Your close relationships are the biggest source of pain and learning. It drives you towards personal growth and spirituality. It is time to be grateful to those experiences and take them in your stride instead of resenting them. You are likely to find a partner in your spiritual journey this month.

July

Work

Your competitors this month will keep you busy as you try to hone your skills and upgrade yourself in your field of work to stay relevant. Work will be good, frustrating at times but mostly fulfilling and satisfying. Networking within your organisation or your field will be helpful in bringing more opportunities. You are also likely to celebrate a milestone this month and be conferred with a reward or recognition.

Finances

Finances are likely to be on your mind this month as you struggle with increasing expenses and unexpected costs. It is good to keep money in mind when taking up projects but too much focus on money can take you away from your purpose and quality work and also make you lose track of your motivation and desire to work with integrity. Dive deeper within you this month to explore the root cause of money issues and plug the leak.

Love

This will be a fruitful month in matters of love as you receive proposals and offers for connection. A new relationship could blossom but it will need some work and time. If you are in a steady relationship, this is the time to set aside your differences and work together towards a single goal. Help is available for you to deal with any relationship challenges. The problems are not big but they need attention and some tweaking.

Relationships

Your relationships need time and patience. Try not to run away from difficult situations but face them. It gets easier with time. There may be some adjustment problems with some new members in the family or with a new situation. Your family will need your attention this month. So you will have to balance your work and personal life to ensure you are able to do justice to both.

Health

Overall health will be good. Get-togethers and social gatherings may take much of your time and also give you opportunities to indulge. Maintain moderation and your health journey will be fine. Don't be too hard on yourself with guilt and anger. Your health goals are within reach right now. Occasional hiccups can be expected but nothing major with regards to health.

Spirituality

You may decide to take up a new spiritual practice or perhaps revive an old one. It will be good for you. Any course of study related to body and mind will be beneficial for you and help you understand yourself much better. This month, take nature walks as a way to sort your mind and calm yourself. Practise active meditation and mindfulness while you are on your nature walk.

August

Work

Work will be good this month. Many opportunities for proving yourself are likely to present themselves and you will be able to make full use of them. You are likely to be involved in multiple projects that will bring you recognition and growth in your professional life. This is a time to be steady and grounded. Work done right now will help you reap benefits for some time to come in the future. This is a fruitful month as many deadlines will be met and projects will be completed.

Finances

Financial situation can be stressful this month as you may find yourself chasing after borrowers and find it difficult to meet your obligations. Your focus will help you ride through the situations and also help you find solutions to your current predicament. Stay away from risky investments but do not be afraid of taking smaller risks. You will be forced to look into your habits of spending and saving this month and rectify or modify some things in your attitude regarding this.

Love

Close intimate relationships may sometimes leave you dumbfounded and confused. Even though you may be giving your best, your partner may feel otherwise. It is important to look at love and relationships from not just your perspective but also from the point of view of your partner's. It is time for some analysis and open conversation about what your partner wants and how you can give it to them.

Relationships

Your relationships need to be handled with care. You may have to balance your time between your work and personal life as your loved ones will demand your attention. Money matters in the family can keep you busy as well as some legal matters may need your attention and focus. Reach out to well-wishers and friends as they can be a great support system at this time. You may get an opportunity to get into business with a family member.

Health

Health is better this month. The changing season may create some problems such as aches and pains, allergies may flare up and general immunity may be low. Spend some time everyday doing something for your health. Even a few minutes and little steps everyday will help. You are on the verge of a breakthrough regarding your health. Keep your hopes up and stay positive.

Spirituality

Family can be a source of love and support as well as a trigger for growth. It is in the moments of peace that personal and spiritual work can be done. The practice helps when there are moments of turmoil. Right now is the time to work on the foundations of your spiritual life. Take some time out everyday to practise mindfulness, awareness and breathing.

September

Work

This is likely to be a very fruitful and successful month professionally. You will be in a good place with recognition and power to create a difference. The old projects are coming to a close and it is time to focus on looking for the next steps. Overseas connections are likely to bring in good business and opportunity. You may feel a sense of completion at your present place of work and are ready to look ahead either in terms of promotion, growth or a new job.

Finances

Financially this is likely to be a better month. The inflows will gradually increase and your ideas related to income are in good order. Your passion about something will convert into material abundance. It is time to follow your purpose and focus on doing your best so that the universe can help you survive and grow. Overall, this is a positive and uplifting month for you financially.

Love

If you are looking for love, this is not the time to pursue love or a relationship relentlessly, rather sit back and focus on what you want and then allow that to move into your life. It does not mean you are not going to do any effort but don't get desperate; the efforts need to be done with a positive intention. You are likely to come across your soulmate this month. If you are in a steady relationship, no matter how long it has been, still take some time to get to know something new about your partner.

Relationships

Overall relationships are likely to be positive this month as you become more assertive about your needs and bring more clarity into your relationships about your boundaries. You are going to be a source of guidance and counsel someone in the family. You will be divinely guided to help them in an emotional manner. This month you are going to meet new people who might become your friends. Some professional connections might turn into personal relationships.

Health

Health will be average. You may find it tiring as you have been relentlessly working towards an improved health and lifestyle. It is okay to take a break sometimes and allow your body to set into a new schedule. This is also a good time to try a new health regimen or a nutritionist to help you ahead in your health plans. Regular exercise is recommended to keep up the rhythm that the body has become used to.

Spirituality

This is a good month to try something new with yourself spiritually, perhaps a new method of meditation or a different energy modality. If you are new to this field, this is a good time to enrol yourself for a course in healing or alternative medicine. Your healing journey begins with accepting your passions and purpose.

October

Work

Quite a few changes are happening at the workplace this month and also in the way you have been working. Even though the changes may be somewhat difficult and come with their own challenges, it is going to be good for you in the long term. Changes in the hierarchy will bring fresh energy in the work environment. If you have been planning to change your field of work, this is a good time to take a step in that direction.

Finances

Finances will be good this month. Money that has been stuck is likely to come in creating more ease for you. This is a good time to plan future investments and begin with investing. Though the inflow and expenses are likely to be similar, yet the promise of money flowing in will make things easier. Do some charity work this month either donating money or services. Bless the money that comes in as well as what goes out.

Love

Your partner will be supportive and loving. You will be able to spend some good quality time with them alone as well as in a group. If you are looking for love, there may be some time before someone shows up and wins your heart. Before that happens, it is important for you to heal any wounds from the past and your disappointments and expectations as well before you get into another relationship.

Relationships

Relationships will need some skill to handle this month. Your insight and awareness will help you deal with people with ease and clarity. It is okay to set strong boundaries if you want to maintain peace of mind and have less drama in life. Your close family will need your time and you will be able to spend some enjoyable moments with them. A young one in the family will benefit from your guidance and teaching.

Health

Health will be good. You may have to multitask this month which can cause some strain on your health. Keeping an attitude of playfulness will help you deal with any situation easily. A vacation at this time can help you destress and refresh your senses. It is time to make efforts towards your health by doing some active body work and connecting to your breath.

Spirituality

Any new spiritual practice started at this time will prove to be beneficial for your mind, body and soul. You may learn from a mentor and guide, associating with an organisation is not the best thing at this time. It is better to take your journey on your own with some guidance. Self study and doing some inner work will be helpful.

November

Work

This month would be about excelling at work, collaborations and establishing your presence. There is likely to be some competition which will propel you to work harder and apply a new approach to your work and the way you handle it. Some conflict at the workplace can happen but it will be handled with ease and wisdom. A lady figure in your life will play an important role in helping you towards your goals.

Finances

Your passion towards your work and being successful and perfect in what you do will help you achieve your financial goals this month. The universe is supporting you in every way to manifest miracles. There may be some doubts regarding your ability to achieve your goal but it is just that, a doubt. You may want to apply a fresh approach to dealing with money this month as the old approach and thinking is not working in a productive manner.

Love

Fear of commitment can stir up strong emotions within you this month as your relationship is moving into a new direction. You may be worried about certain things said and done and want to escape the consequences instead of facing them. But there is nothing that love cannot solve. The situation is not as bad as you imagine it to be. There could be a breakdown in communication and will need your efforts to resuscitate. Focus on joy and goodness instead of fears and doom.

Relationships

. You have been working on creating better boundaries in your relationships and this has resulted in you understanding what is okay and acceptable and what is not. This understanding will help you navigate the landscape of every challenging relationship and deal with difficult people as well. Something beautiful is coming soon in your personal life, stay hopeful and optimistic. Nurture the goodness in your relationships by acknowledging and working on it.

Health

Health will be good. There is a sense of robustness and strength that will support you in your endeavours this month. You know what is working and what can help you further. Your ideas are good but need a little more research. In the meanwhile, stay steady on your course and enjoy the results of your hard work. Activity and keeping your mind busy will be helpful at this time.

Spirituality

Patience and service are the key factors for your spiritual growth this month. As you focus on serving others with the gifts you have been bestowed upon, the path to your own spiritual growth opens up with clarity. Meanwhile, take it easy. Don't rush into anything. There is no need to hurry or force things to happen. Everything is occurring in perfect timing.

December

Work

Your creative juices are flowing and work will be good. You are focussed and determined towards achieving your goals and will likely achieve them in time. This is a good time to work towards being an entrepreneur or a position in your organisation that you have had your eyes upon. But things will take time, do not rush them. Don't try to take any shortcuts as they can backfire in a bad way. Do your work diligently. Remember, slow and steady wins the race.

Finances

Finances will be good overall. You have been working hard and it is paying you well. But this is not the time to rest. You will need to keep up your momentum so that the wheel keeps turning. Any loans that you had been waiting for will be cleared. A sudden expense this month can throw you off balance. So keep an eye out for emergencies and keep some liquidity with you. Don't tie up all your funds in assets.

Love

Even though love is coming your way, yet you sometimes turn your head away to not look at it. Your past experiences are colouring your present and not letting you enjoy the moment. Not every relationship will be as bad. So take chances, you have a lot of good people coming to you. If you are in a relationship, you may want to do some ground work in communion and understanding your partner's love language to smooth any wrinkles.

Relationships

Relationships have been a cause of concern and stress for some time. But things are getting better as you learn to handle people and situations and set healthy boundaries. However, mentally you are still imagining the worst and finding faults in others' intentions. This is not the best way for you right now as you are seeing people from a lens of fear and mistrust. Heal your wounds and open your heart. You are only limited by your fears. There are many good people out there.

Health

Health is good. Your new regimen is working for you. As you lighten up your worries and adopt a playful attitude in life, your stress levels become more manageable. It will positively impact your health. Seek out alternative healers to help you with regulating your emotions and physical body. Dance, movement and nature will be very healing for you this month. Focus on what is working and look forward to good health instead of time you lost when you were not in good shape.

Spirituality

There are things about you that are coming to light. You may not find them appealing but they have been a part of you nonetheless. Embrace these shadow aspects. Spirituality is not just all the good things and good vibes. It means wading through the mud of the human psyche to discover the lotus. Universe is helping you with signs and messages to guide you towards healing, embracing and freeing yourself from your fears.

CHAPTER EIGHT

Libra

September 23–October 23

Overview

The theme of 2023 is overcoming your limiting beliefs and expressing your authentic self with courage and freedom. This year will be about dealing with your fears that stop you from succeeding, giving your hundred percent to life and having the courage to take bold steps. You will take risks, find your footing in the world and explore new territories both physically and mentally.

The key to accomplish your dreams successfully is in your hands and you will realise it this year very clearly. Librans are always seeking as is significant from your zodiac symbol which is a balance. This year stability will be a theme, you will be grounded enough to have the patience to work towards your goals.

Working in teams, collaboration, enjoying with friends, creating something new in partnerships will happen. This is not a year of solitude and individual growth, but collective growth for you. You have been through changes and shifts in the past year and this year you will be propelled towards networking and connecting with more people.

Personally, this is going to be an interesting year as you engage with people from all your heart, open yourself to new connections and connect with your family, friends and loved ones increasingly from a loving and secure space. You are likely to see many changes still going on both personally and professionally. In your professional life, you are likely to play the role of a coach and mentor for people helping them in their growth and success. This in turn will help you grow and prosper.

First half of the year is going to be about changes, the old giving way to the new. It can be a confusing and difficult time occasionally, but eventually as the dust settles, you will begin to see glimpses of a new era, a new phase in your life. The second half of the year will bring in new projects, people and creative ventures. This will be a great time to establish your business, expand, and bring in new business entities under your banner. For creative professionals, this is going to be a beautiful time as your creativity will be at its peak and you will find expression of it very satisfying and rewarding.

January

Work

Work this month will be about partnerships, teams and collaborations. You will work efficiently and productively along with people and the project/venture will be enjoyable and successful. If you are trying to do a side hustle, it may not be as fruitful this month. Any freelancing work may not give you much opportunity or rewards. So take your time choosing the right thing to work on. You may feel as if you won't be compensated fairly in a mutual partnership agreement but it is coming more from your fears than anything else.

Finances

You are likely to have plenty of opportunity and sources of income this month for you to choose from. It will be literally like wish fulfilment. But your fears and attitude of lack and worries can put a damper on your future plans. Making a decision is likely to be tough this month in regards to finances. But there is really nothing to worry about. You are being guided well, listen to it. You don't have to do it all alone.

Love

In matters of love, perhaps you are thinking too much and not feeling enough. You are looking at relationships from a standpoint of what you will get rather than also thinking about what you bring to the table. The give and take has to be equal enough to make a difference. You also need to keep your expectations from your partner more realistic otherwise it can lead to frustration and your partner feeling like they bear all the burden of the relationship.

Relationships

Relationships are a matter of heart but some people around you are being inauthentic, hypocritical and deceitful about their intentions. It is best not to engage in it as it will only cause more stress and no real gain. If you are looking to start a business with a family member, make sure you and them are committed enough to see it through. You need to be more practical in certain relationships and trust your insights.

Health

Health will be good this month. There may be some minor complaints of heat related problems that may cause skin issues and stress headaches. This will be a good time to plan and begin a health regimen that has been on your mind for some time now. Progress will be good. You may experience resistance but you will be able to deal with it.

Spirituality

One often finds themselves swinging to extreme polar opposites before finding a balance. Give yourself the liberty to go through that process. Your quest for balance will help you find your truth and accept others' truths as well. Spend time in nature to stabilise your moods and help you with regulating your body clock and natural rhythms.

February

Work

You will be sharp, focussed and have the clarity that will help you do your work with excellence and meet your deadlines as well. You may feel the burden of work and may even feel overworked at times. Learn to delegate the routine tasks to someone so that you can focus on what's important. A partnership offer will be exciting and lucrative. If you have been waiting or looking forward to something like that, then it is time to consider it seriously.

Finances

Finances will be good and the financial situation will be stable this month. You are likely to invest your money in enhancing your skills and upgrading yourself for your work. It will pay good dividends in the future. There may be some impulsive spending which will seem to be unnecessary but it will help enhance your enthusiasm for work and life. Caution from the cards is to not follow the money but follow your passion otherwise you may land in trouble.

Love

Your luck may be down in matters of love this month. A breakup or a disappointment from a partner can pull you off track. You will need time and patience to deal with it. It may even be a breakup that happened in the past and still is haunting you and preventing you from creating beautiful relationships. It is time to move on and allow your heart to feel the love again. If you are in a relationship, it is going through some changes. Embrace the change so that it becomes easier to accept.

Relationships

Your relationships have undergone a change or are changing. You will learn to create better boundaries which will help you deal with different relationships in a much better manner. Listen to your heart, follow your intuition about people and act accordingly. You don't need to put up pretences for people to like and accept you. The ones who resonate with you will like you no matter what.

Health

In matters of health there is likely to be a tug of war between your body and your body intelligence. Your body follows the conditioning it has received about food and health no matter what. But your body intelligence knows exactly what's beneficial and what's harmful for you. This month, you will need to pay particular attention to this subtle voice of intelligence and follow it otherwise your health could suffer.

Spirituality

The unseen often takes hold of our imagination. We either romance it or are scared of it. This month you may face situations whose outcomes may be unpredictable. It can be a cause of concern and worry. But know that the universe plays fair. Whether something is fair according to you or not, the universe is always fair and just. This will be a time to acknowledge your fear of uncertainty and work on building trust in the universe.

March

Work

As your current projects come to a close, you will be on the lookout for new ventures or clients. But there is likely to be a delay in the new work or project. Meanwhile, tie any loose ends, find closure with the jobs done and connect with your colleagues to celebrate even the minor victories and successes. It is a good time to look for new opportunities overseas. However, the new is going to take some time and patience to come. In the meantime, work on your dream project and nurture it with more energy.

Finances

Finances will be good overall this month. Old sources of income may dry up. But it should not be a cause for concern as new doors are opening for you. New avenues for growth, income and investments are on the horizon. This is a good time to seek expert opinion for managing your finances and investments. You may choose to close bad debts this month. Your ideas for money are worthwhile, put them into practice.

Love

Librans are seemingly often torn between two parts of themselves. This is also the energy that will show up in matters of love this month as new love enters your life but at the same time, the critical and analytical part of you activates trying to figure out all the red flags. Relationships are not projects. That is all you need to remember this month and spare yourself excessive analysis and thoughts.

Relationships

There are people in your family and friend circle who support and love you. Yet at times you tend to feel isolated and rejected, second guessing yourself if they want you or not. You don't have to be needed by someone for them to love you. This is perhaps the biggest learning for you this year. Good times with friends and family are on the cards. You are also looked upon as a wise one who can help people with their problems. Don't be surprised if someone from the extended family reaches out to you.

Health

Health wise, you have seen better days. This month may not be one of those. You may experience random aches and pains, mostly due to elevated levels of air energy in the body. There is also a lot of thinking which is draining your energy and making you feel lethargic. Plug those leaks in your energy and psyche and you will see a remarkable difference in your health issues. Consult an energy healer for advice and help if needed.

Spirituality

A healthy give and take constitutes the law of nature. But if you just keep giving and don't receive, you will end up being an empty swamp. This is a time when you need to learn to give and receive as well. Ask others to help you instead of trying to do everything on your own. Allow yourself to receive. This will open up your intuition and energy and ability to give to others with love.

April

Work

This is a month for you to show up in your authentic self, give your best to your work and reap its benefits. Any time you shirk your responsibilities even if it is because you think you are not good enough or capable enough, it creates negative karma. You will need to act decisively and fast this month to make the most of opportunities that present themselves to you. Otherwise you may regret them. Trust the universe to bring you the best and help you give your hundred percent.

Finances

You may want to experiment with certain investment strategies this month. Although it is a good idea, it may cause you or others around you some trouble. So be careful and cautious. It is okay to take risks, but not at the expense of someone else. Your heart and gut is in the right place. Finances will be smooth this month and it is advisable to play risky games with only the surplus.

Love

In matters of love, this month is likely to be a good and optimistic time. If you are looking for love, you may want to have realistic expectations. If you feel too emotional or acting from fear around someone, (even an attitude of wanting an upper hand comes from fear), take it as a red flag. If you are in a steady relationship, this will be a good time to spend some happy moments with your partner and perhaps even take a vacation.

Relationships

You are likely to shine in your family and you will be in demand. But not all those who appreciate your success are your well-wishers. Keep this in mind when sharing your intimate details with someone. Stay hopeful as you will meet someone who will turn out to be a very good friend. But the path to that goes through uncertainty about people and the ability to trust someone. Remember, when in doubt, trust your gut.

Health

Health will be good overall. The burden of work and looking after your health, especially if dealing with an illness, can cause you to feel stressed and overwhelmed. But know that you are on the right track. The efforts you are making are working. You may want to take a second opinion or seek out an alternative health professional to help you with your issues. Spending some time alone in the presence of animals will be very therapeutic.

Spirituality

Every habit, belief and pattern begins with a seed of thought. This is the right time to sow the seeds of whatever it is you want in your life. Practising affirmations, having the clarity of what you want and trusting the process of manifesting will go a long way in creating the kind of life you want. But it all begins with the seed and the clarity of your intent.

May

Work

Work this month will be good. A partnership is likely to come your way which will be fruitful. But this is maybe not the best time to get into entrepreneurship. Get more clarity about your business plan and think ahead before jumping ship. You may be planning to go for higher studies or enhancing your skill set. This is the right time to do that. A professional course will be beneficial for your career growth.

Finances

Finances will be good this month. You are focussed and your dedication to your financial goals will play a major part in helping you achieve them. Don't let your fears stop you from taking some calculated risks. This is perhaps not the best time to invest your money in assets. Keep some liquidity with you for day to day running of business and work. Avoid lending money to anyone this month as it may not come back.

Love

You seem to be assuming the worst in matters of love. Perhaps some optimism will help you overcome your negative thinking. Don't make your relationships into power games or mind plays as it will only hurt your partner and your relationship. You may feel uncertain in a relationship regarding your status, this is not the right time to clarify this. The clarity you really need is within you first about what you want.

Relationships

Relationships will be good and give you much joy and hope. You will need to take out time from your busy schedule for your friends and family this month. It is important to give time to an important aspect of your life. Spending happy times with friends is on the cards. You can drop your guard around your family and be a little goofy as well. It keeps the happiness quotient high and also helps you destress.

Health

Your health will be good. Energy levels will be high helping you in your day-to-day activities. If you have been thinking of a new health regimen to help improve your energy and fitness levels, this is a good time to get started with it. Only thinking about it is not going to work. Indulge in some playful activities or sports with your loved ones. It will help you bond with them more and also provide you a good workout.

Spirituality

You have been trying to patch your heart and push any wounds under the carpet. This helps you to deal with life everyday but it is not very healthy for you as it keeps the wound open and unhealed through which poison and toxicity can seep into your mind and life. Take some time to really heal yourself emotionally and spiritually. It is okay to ask for help with this.

June

Work

This month you are likely to be light hearted and a little easy going at work. You will experiment with ideas and be open to new opportunities or job offers. If you are just starting your career, this is perhaps the time to focus on learning on the job rather than focus on money. This is a crucial time for you to enhance your skills and apprentice with someone to learn new methods. You may feel distracted more often and will need to remind yourself of deadlines to help you pull through.

Finances

Financially this will be a good month. You are likely to receive pending payments for your work and rewards for your performance. Choose to invest your money in safe instruments and begin investing now if you haven't yet started. Practise a moderate approach to spending as you could be tempted to spend blindly this month. Don't worry too much about little things related to money, have an open heart.

Love

Your relationship will be fine and is even likely to be smooth. Yet you are thinking too much, perhaps imagining the worst. The past is over and as long as you have healed it and act with awareness in your relationship and love matters, it won't repeat. If you have gone through a breakup and it was painful, take time to heal it. Don't intellectualise it and jump into a new relationship so soon.

Relationships

Even though relationships are fine and there is peace around you, yet you seem to be going through a storm internally. Something from the past may be bothering you or perhaps you are not able to resonate with people around you as your frequencies are changing. Perspectives change for the better, but that does not mean you have to find new people, you can start shifting the dynamics with the people around you gradually too. You will receive love and support from your loved ones.

Health

Health will be good. You may indulge yourself in excessive food and drinks at get-togethers with friends as well as family. Stay watchful of that. Also excessive socialising can leave you feeling drained and tired. Take some time out with yourself doing things you like or maybe even just meditating and being in silence. A solo trip to the mountains or a peaceful place can be rejuvenating.

Spirituality

You are going through an enormous transformation right now which brings blessings. But it can be a challenge to deal with the world simultaneously. You may want to be alone in your world as you go through this change, but the social life may be unavoidable. Seek out people who are either going through the same phase or have already been, they can help guide you through this phase.

July

Work

You will need to safeguard and protect your projects this month. You have done good work and this is the time to move ahead with it. Don't let the past prevent you from growing and moving ahead. A change in your workplace, job, type of business or even in the way you approach work is likely to change in a big way this month. Don't be too attached to what was, rather flow with the change. It won't be as painful as you are imagining.

Finances

This month will be a new beginning of sorts when it comes to finances. Your ideas for creating abundance are good and valuable. You hold the seeds in your hands for it. It is time to plant them. As you nurture them, they will grow into steady income. This is a good time to create passive income sources as well. You have the skill and the mindset to create this new stream of income.

Love

Even though love is coming to you, yet you seem to be immersed in your life, work and you tend to stick to your way of thinking and life. If you are looking for marriage, good proposals are likely to come your way. Analyse them before moving ahead with any one. Your current relationship needs time and some effort. It is important to nurture what you have so that it does not wither away.

Relationships

You may find relationships somewhat challenging this month. You have changed and consequently the quality of your connection and the dynamic therein also is changing. You may find it difficult to connect with certain people in the family as they can be resistant to the new you and want the same old you to be present. It may be that both you and the other person need time to adjust to this shift. Don't be too harsh on yourself and don't expect others to change at the pace that you have.

Health

Health is likely to be better. But you may experience some distress in the body. It is not likely to be anything physical but has its roots in emotional turmoil and disturbance. You have all the right resources to deal with it. But just don't ignore it. This may be time for you to start looking at health and healing from a completely different perspective and stop separating mind, body and soul. You have to treat all to achieve holistic health.

Spirituality

It is said that when the student is ready, the teacher appears. Perhaps you are ready now because you are going to meet someone who will be your guide and guru in your spiritual healing journey. Don't take spirituality too seriously. That is not what it is about. The more playful you are, the easier the journey gets. Take some quiet time meditating, perhaps find a retreat centre which can help you with this.

August

Work

As some projects or ventures come to a close this month, you may feel a sense of loss of purpose and motivation. Participating in a professional networking event will be fruitful at this time. If you have doubted your capabilities for carrying out your responsibilities, this month will provide you ample evidence for the contrary. Connect to your purpose and follow your passion as it will give you a renewed sense of direction.

Finances

You may indulge in financial deals this month which will be a win-win situation for both the parties. Remember to complete the give and take and be discerning about who you give your money or make someone in charge of your investments. If you have been looking for expanding or adding sources of income to your portfolio, then this is the right time to work in that direction. You may choose to do something unrelated to your field of work for this as well.

Love

If you are looking for love, it may take some time to manifest in your life. Use this opportunity to work on your relationship patterns. If you are in a steady relationship, you will enjoy spending some quality time with your partner and children. Indulging in mutually enjoyable activities, even adventure sports can be a good outlet for energies and an opportunity to bond. You may have to find time for your partner as work can keep you busy.

Relationships

This month you may find it difficult to connect with people in the family as you used to. This may cause you some disappointment and nostalgia. You will need to be careful about who you trust your secrets with in friends and family as not all you see may be true. This is also a good time to discern who is a part of your inner circle and who is not. You may be guided to strengthen your personal boundaries and have clarity about this.

Health

Health will be good overall. You may experience occasional aches and pains and stiffness in the body. Be careful in your workouts as there are chances of an injury. Make sure you do sufficient warm ups and cool downs before and after. This may be a good time to do some research into a suitable lifestyle for you. You may even seek out an expert opinion in this regard.

Spirituality

You may want to move ahead or progress in your spiritual journey. But remember, this journey is always one step forward and two steps back. So have patience and keep yourself focussed towards your personal practices. This is a good time for detoxing your mind and body to help you come into a better state for meditation and spiritual growth.

September

Work

You may experience some competitiveness and conflicts at your workplace this month. This may prove to be a hurdle in meeting your deadlines or getting work done smoothly. It is recommended to keep egos in check and establish clear communication and resolve conflicts before they become major issues. You may be involved in studies to upgrade yourself by attending workshops and conferences. You may meet an old professional contact with whom you shared a good bond and this will bring back all the memories you made working together.

Finances

Financially this month may not be as fruitful as you had expected. Even though you are focussed on your work, there may be some hiccups with payments. It is time to apply a new approach in financial matters as the old one is not working any more. You may experience an increased self doubt regarding your capabilities and find yourself not being able to make use of the current opportunities to make money. Pay attention to this and deal with it before it starts creating bigger problems.

Love

You may experience some problems with your partner and things may deteriorate to the point of a breakdown in relationship or marriage. But this is not the time to take any extreme actions. Give yourself and your partner some cool down time and then resume your discussion. The issue is not so huge that it can disrupt a beautiful bond. Things can be sorted out. Focus on the blessings instead of what is not there or what you lost in your relationship and life in general.

Relationships

Your relationships will be pleasant as you navigate them with wisdom and clarity. You are a steady rock for someone in your life. You may even find your anchor and some stability in your relationships this month. It is a good time to seek wisdom and learnings from an elder in your family or an expert who can guide you in this area.

Health

Health will be good overall this month. Your health program, if any that you are following, is getting you results. This is a time to conserve your energies. Social interactions and conflict can scatter your energies which can cause low immunity and other health problems eventually. Gather your energies by going out in nature, choose your battles wisely and heal your fears. You may keep worrying about something being wrong with you. Get a health checkup and get some peace of mind.

Spirituality

You are being called to pursue your passion. Be honest with yourself, what is your heart's true desire? What gives you happiness and motivation? If you find yourself confused and lost, connect with the energies of the Sun and open your heart to receiving wisdom and inspiration.

October

Work

This month you may not be in a mood to focus on your work. But the workload will be heavy and you will need to pull up your socks to meet the deadlines. This is a good month to spend on doing things slowly and steadily so that you don't compromise on the quality and the work also gets done eventually. A long awaited reward or a due promotion is likely to happen this month.

Finances

Finances will be good this month. You are likely to make some impulse purchases, so caution is advised. You are not focussed on money but on doing things that bring you peace of mind. This is a good approach as long as you don't spend your hard earned money blindly. A partnership proposal will bring abundance and fortune.

Love

A proposal may come from a friend who secretly likes you. This is overall a good month if you are looking for love. If you are in a ready relationship, you may be thinking about how you want to show up in your relationship as your past conditioning dictates something but your heart guides you to something else. You may be torn between being dominant and needy and co-existing as friends. Choosing the latter approach is healthy for your relationship.

Relationships

In terms of relationships, this month will be calm and peaceful. You are most likely to be in a hermit mode wanting to spend time with yourself or only with close loved ones. Social life may feel draining and too much for your senses right now. Friends and family are forthcoming and are willing to support you in your ventures and way of life. This is a good time to connect with a dear one with whom you had lost touch.

Health

Health will be good this month. There may be occasional health issues mostly related to gut problems. You will need to pay attention to your diet and body intelligence. It is possible what the general wisdom says may not help you as much as the ancient wisdom. Do some research on this to find what's best for you.

Spirituality

You are good at helping, counselling and healing young adults and children. Use your skills to help children. You are being guided well by your mentor or the inner guru. The calling that you experience on the inside beckons you to follow your heart's purpose. In helping others, you are helping yourself.

November

Work

The pace of work will be slow and can get frustrating at times. This is the time to incubate and plan projects and future ventures. The things that you are working on will take some time to reach completion. Keep nurturing them. Don't force anything to happen as it can backfire. This is also a time for major changes at the workplace. The structure and hierarchy is undergoing shifts which can be difficult to deal with initially. This is a good time for a job or a career change.

Finances

Take your time to plan your moves and investments. Do not rush into any decisions right now. There may be some confusion or uncertainty in your mind. This is the right time to consult someone who knows the field that you wish to invest in. Any rash decisions can be counter productive. Your plans and ideas are good. But don't get too influenced by what others say. Their experience need not be your reality.

Love

Love and relationships will be a source of comfort and safety for you this month. For those in a steady relationship, you will be able to spend quality time with your partner, you may even participate in mutually enjoyable activities and social gatherings. Your partner will support you in every way in your financial and professional matters. If you are seeking love, this is a good time to get your intentions right, bring some clarity into what you want and actively seek out.

Relationships

Relationships will be pleasant. A family gathering will be peaceful and fruitful. Matters of inheritance may take some time but will be resolved without much difficulty and animosity. A trip with friends is likely to happen and it will refresh your senses and be enjoyable. If you have been planning to move abroad with family, this is a good time to broach the subject and work towards it.

Health

If you are recovering from an injury, you need to give yourself enough rest to heal. Don't try to push your body otherwise it can worsen the injury and delay the healing process. You can be in as good health as you really want. If you are planning a diet program or fitness routine, you need to first get enough motivation and be really interested in achieving your goal. Work with a coach or an expert for help with this.

Spirituality

One of the myths of the modern world is independent existence. Human beings are social animals and do well in groups. If you are looking to be detached, it does not mean you don't need anyone, it means you need to depend on yourself for your needs but be interdependent for your social requirements. It is good to have someone to share your life with. But it begins by creating your own life.

December

Work

Work will be fulfilling and satisfying as you are able to bag that lucrative project or client that you had been pursuing for some time now. A celebration of sorts is on the cards. Find time to hang out with your professional colleagues and associates as it helps with networking as well. This is the time to have clarity about your goals and how you can achieve them. This will provide you motivation and inspiration and ignite your passion towards your work.

Finances

Finances are good and will be sufficient for your needs this month. You have the ability to attract more and have financial freedom. But your money beliefs, like money is evil or it corrupts, interfere with your ability to achieve your financial goals. Someone around you cannot be trusted with money matters and you need to be careful this month. You may be sitting on a gold mine and yet be thinking if you can dig it. Let go of your hesitation and doubts and work towards achieving the holy grail.

Love

You are likely to be nostalgic about your past relationships or how things were in the past. This is going to create more problems and unhappiness for you and your partner or would be partner. This attitude is not letting you see the good that you have with you and will create bitterness and feelings of regret. Things change, life changes, so do relationships. The sooner you accept this, and be grateful for what you have, the better it will be for you and your relationships.

Relationships

This month you may be worried about a young one in the family and be concerned over matters of their education and focus. Instead of worrying and radiating the vibes of stress, tackle the situation wisely. You have the skills to manage people and get the best out of them. Do not coerce but persuade through love and your wit.

Health

Health will be good this month as you take your responsibilities to work on your fitness seriously. A partner in your health journey, it could be your lover, spouse, trainer or even a nutritionist, will help you move towards your goals effortlessly. You may indulge at parties or at family gatherings. Don't feel guilty, just get back to your routine the next day. Recovery from an illness is on the cards.

Spirituality

You may find expression through an art form this month which will bring your soul a lot of joy. Don't get too carried away though and don't start planning your future in it. Take it as a joyful activity, enjoy the moments you spend indulging in it. The moment you start thinking ahead, it takes the fun out of it and then there is no soul left in the work.

CHAPTER NINE

Scorpio

October 24–November 21

Overview

The theme of 2023 for Scorpios is seeking balance - between feminine and masculine aspects of your personality, between work and personal life, giving and receiving, work and rest etc. The year brings opportunities and abundance along with happiness and joy of family, relationships and friends.

There may be a tendency for you to indulge in one aspect to the extreme, often at the cost of others. This is where seeking balance will play a major role. You are sharp, focussed and have a no nonsense attitude. This will be highlighted this year as you navigate the landscape of your professional and personal life.

You are passionate about a lot of things, but more than that you are fiercely protective about the close loved ones in your life. This tendency will need to be checked as it could create possible issues in your relationships. Your foresight this year will help you make the right decisions in every aspect of your life. A trip overseas is on the cards this year.

Your personal life will be fulfilling and a course of comfort for you. Your fierceness to protect your loved ones comes from you feeling them as a part of you. You will be a warm host but would like to spend your time in close company of a selected few that are a part of your inner circle. Your professional life will be dotted with success and your ability to create a stable position. This year, anything you want will be manifested with ease.

First half of the year will see you working hard towards your dreams, projects and giving your more than a hundred percent. But it will also bring results and rewards in correlation to your work. Don't be afraid of challenges, take calculated risks and stay grounded. The second half of the year may see you hesitant and uncertain about things in your personal life. A few skeletons may tumble out of the closet forcing you to face them and deal with them once and for all.

January

Work

The flow of work will be smooth this month. Though many opportunities for work, projects and jobs will come to you, yet you seem to be in a mood for contemplation. You will want to tie up the loose ends and complete your pending projects before taking on any new work. Though this is a good approach, it tends to make you thorough and also gives you a chance to think about the kind of work you want, but remember that opportunity may not knock again. So consider the options before it's too late.

Finances

Your financial issues may keep bothering you at times this month. But given your efforts to get things in flow, your worries may soon become a thing of the past. You may be worried about taking care of yourself and your family and responsibilities, but you worry in vain. You will be able to overcome any challenges and come into abundance. You may be urged to make some major financial decisions this month.

Love

You will be lucky in matters of love this month. If you are looking for a life mate, you are likely to meet suitable people and matches this month. Connect to your inner wisdom and remember your learnings from past relationships when making any decision regarding this. If you are in a steady relationship, you will be able to connect with your lover on a deeper level. Mutual respect and love are the cornerstones of a happy relationship.

Relationships

You will find comfort and happiness in the company of close friends and loved ones. A get together of friends this month will give you the opportunity to enjoy your time as well as bond with them better. You are likely to expand your social circle this month as you seek out like minded people to connect with. If someone in the friends and family has hurt you, you don't need to hold any grudge in your heart, karma will take care of it. Just learn your lesson and move on so it doesn't repeat.

Health

Health will be good as your efforts are rewarded. You are likely to follow a health and fitness routine that will help you achieve your health goals. You may get attracted to a fad fitness regimen, but look into it deeply before you actually begin to follow it as it may not be the right thing for you. You may experience some stiffness in the body and digestion related issues this month. Hydration, fibre and flexible thinking can help you deal with it effectively.

Spirituality

You don't have to be in a rat race to feel normal or to fit in. It is time to recognise your own goals and qualities that will help in your spiritual journey. You need to tailor your spiritual discipline and practices to your particular personality, traits and goals. Seek a mentor's guidance in this matter to help you. This is a good time to detox your mind and body through holistic health practices like yoga and a vegetarian diet.

February

Work

The month will have periods of intense activity and then times of complete lack of action. You will need to juggle your mind and make use of both the phases. When you don't have much to do besides wait for the feedback or next steps, instead of getting worked up about being still, spend that time connecting with fellow workers and completing your pending tasks.

Finances

Finances will be good this month. Some debts would be cleared as a result of your meticulous planning. Investing in partnership can yield good results, but there will still be a need to clear up the misunderstanding and look forward to achieving similar goals. The expenditures will be high but they will be offset by incomes from different sources. This is not the time to dwell in the past but look ahead and plan for the future.

Love

In matters of love, this month can be tricky. If you are looking for love, it might be difficult to understand the true intentions of the other person. Remember, if things seem too good to be true, they probably are. Even if you have an iota of doubt, pay attention to it lest to end up making a deal with the devil. This is a time to stay cautious about your dating habits.

Relationships

You will need to be thorough about any dealings with someone in the family related to money, inheritance or work. It will make sure you don't end up feeling duped or disappointed in the future. You may feel a strain in the relationship with someone in the family. It is better to maintain distance right now than try to proactively do something about it. Some things are better left to time. Avoid taking any rash decisions.

Health

Health will be average. You may experience bouts of seasonal flu and general exhaustion. You may want to spend some time alone with yourself. Don't be too hard on yourself and don't fight with your body. It is okay to let the body indulge and give it what it needs in terms of nutrition, exercise and time. Beaches and water bodies will have a healing effect on you.

Spirituality

You have been worrying too much and trying too hard to make things happen a certain way. But when it doesn't happen, it's not that your efforts were not in the right direction but that it wasn't the time or the best thing for you. Everything is working out as it should. This month is about learning to surrender your worries as well as control.

March

Work

You are likely to be very busy and loaded with work this month so much so that you may end up feeling burnt out or exhausted. New ideas are taking root and fresh opportunities are coming your way. This is the time when you can't afford to say no. Recognition and promotion are on the cards. This is the time to work quietly on your projects without saying or announcing it. If you have been planning to start a business, this is the right time.

Finances

Finances will be good but they will only be enough to begin your projects. You may feel stuck between making a choice between which projects to kick start and invest in. Your ideas for investment and future are good but they need more groundwork. Either do the work at grassroots yourself or tie up with someone who is genuinely willing to do it. This is the time to sow the seeds, not to think of reaping a quick profit.

Love

An old relationship that has lost the spark or emotional bond or an old way of relating to your lover is coming to an end. You will be forced to make a decision soon. This is not a problem that you can find a way out through a loophole. You will have to get in touch with your feelings and do the right thing. There is no need to worry as good things are coming in the future. Contrary to what you may believe, there is goodness and hope ahead.

Relationships

Relationships will be a source of comfort and stability for you this month as you struggle with some important issues in your love life. You may be involved in socialising and hosting get-togethers. These can be beneficial for your professional growth as well. A few friendships that have run their course and are no longer good for you will come to a close.

Health

Health will be average. You will need to pay attention and proactively work on it. Periods of rest will be needed to deal with recurrent allergies or seasonal health issues. Invest in your health this month as a means of preventive care.

Spirituality

You know you are moving in the right direction spiritually when you begin to encounter some resistance to your consistent spiritual practices. You will receive information downloads this month that will help you navigate your spiritual journey's landscape and also be able to help others with their issues related to life. There is no need to play small. You don't have to know everything or be an expert to be able to help someone in their difficult times.

April

Work

Workplace this month can elicit a variety of emotions from frustration and anger to disappointment and hope. A minor tussle with a colleague or a superior can turn into a path altering event. You don't have to react in extremes yet keeping an open eye and an open mind will help you go through this experience without feeling defeated. Options for jobs and other opportunities are likely to come to you but this month you may feel like romancing the idea of entrepreneurship. Take it with a pinch of salt as you explore this idea.

Finances

Finances will be good. There is a need to look at the future sources of income this month. You may have to be a bit more thorough and cautious about your expenditure and curb any leakage as it will affect your future requirements. Your ideas regarding your money management are excellent. They just need precise application.

Love

This is a good month pertaining to relationships and love. You are on the lookout for a suitable partner. The clarity with which you are approaching this right now is going to help you with screening and finding the one who adds value to your life. Looking for marriage proposals will be fruitful. If you are in a relationship, you will need some alone time for yourself. This is imperative for your peace of mind which directly affects the quality of your relationship.

Relationships

Relationships, including friendships, will be beautiful, provide you joy and happiness. An addition to the family is on the cards. You are likely to meet someone after a long time and this meeting will give you a lot of joy. Get-togethers with friends will be fun and provide the necessary distraction and refresh your mind and senses. Overall the energies for relationships this month are heartwarming.

Health

Health will need time and attention and a proactive approach. If there is something you have been ignoring related to health and have had a nagging feeling about it, this is the time to get it looked at. It may be nothing major, but may need some care and remedy. It is beneficial for you to read about foods and exercises that will benefit your particular constitution. There is no reason to worry, instead start looking after your health as you would look after a loved one.

Spirituality

There are times when we can be confused about love and attachment and can tend to think of the latter as love. This is a good time to explore unconditional love and attachments. Attachment is born out of fear whereas love is who you are in your true essence. Love will always be kind and set you free, but attachment will bind you under a heavy weight. The opposite of attachment is not detachment but freedom. You and your relationships blossom in freedom not in attachment.

May

Work

This month will bring fresh opportunities for work. You will need to brace yourself for the overload of work as well as decisions. Your network of contacts is likely to bring you new projects or clients. An overseas opportunity is also on the cards. This month you may have to do the juggling act as you may need to work on multiple projects or clients at the same time causing you to feel exhilarated as well as exhausted.

Finances

Finances may seem to slow down this month. Payments might get delayed. Stay away from investing in schemes that look too good to be true because they probably are. You can end up losing money as well as your own trust. Listen to your instincts. Don't play too risky in the markets this month as it can be uncertain and end up in losses for you. Calculated risks of low measure are okay.

Love

You know in your heart when a relationship is right for you and when it's getting toxic. All that remains is for you to act upon that wisdom. You may try to talk yourself out of it but the truth is, you will need to just listen to your instinct and act on it. If you are in a steady relationship, you may feel that you don't have much to connect over and find it boring or as if the spark has died. Physical intimacy can only help to an extent, but the connection is always more than that. Look for it.

Relationships

You are in a good place right now in terms of relating to people and holding on to those who really matter. You may have to be a little stubborn this month and not give too much benefit of doubt to people around you. The right people will stay and the ones who you no longer resonate with will leave peacefully if you will allow it. This is the time to assert your boundaries even with the family members.

Health

Health will be average as you struggle to balance your life in different aspects. This can take a toll on your mental peace leading you to feel a bit under the weather. Keep up with the practices for good health and lifestyle as they are working for you. Meditation and nature walks will help lower stress levels providing you a sense of calm and relief.

Spirituality

You are in a stable position spiritually, which essentially means you will be grounded, centred and will be able to take decisions from a space of calmness and wisdom. You are likely to guide someone around you into taking their initial steps into the spiritual journey. If that inspires you, put your heart's wish out there in the universe and let it bring you more of that.

June

Work

Work this month could be erratic. You may be more involved with office politics and administrative work than actual productive work. There is a need for clarity this month regarding your goals, how you work and what kind of environment you want at your workplace. There are likely to be many doubts about your own self and capabilities that you may be tempted to look for more courses to enhance your skills. But that's not what you really need. You need clarity and focus, away from politics and you need to look at the bigger picture.

Finances

This is a lucky month regarding finances. Pending payments may be released, loans that were stuck are likely to be sanctioned and you will be able to move ahead with your plans for your future course of action. This is the time to plan ahead so that when you are ready, you can immediately take action on it. A hike is soon going to come your way.

Love

This is the time to look within and heal your inner child for any abandonment wounds, so that you don't carry that baggage into your relationships. You tend to have many expectations from your partner about emotional support without realising the real kind of support that you want, no one else can give you. If you have been struggling in a relationship, this is the time to take charge and responsibility for your happiness and do something about it.

Relationships

You may experience a loss or a sense of it this month. It is important that you seek emotional or mental health support to cope with your feelings, even if it is the loss of a friendship or a relationship. Do not try to run away from what you feel but do not keep wallowing in the feelings all the time as well. Neither approach is healthy. Take some time out and connect to your friends and family for support.

Health

Health will be good. Your efforts towards improving your fitness levels and healing any health issues will be rewarded. Working with an instructor or coach will be helpful this month as they can guide and inspire you to achieve your health goals. If recovering from an illness, it will be expedited with positive thinking and visualisation.

Spirituality

You may not be able to spend too much time for yourself and your spiritual practices which can end up making you feel guilty. But remember, spirituality is an aspect of who you are and it is an attitude, a perspective of life. Focus on all the things you do everyday - in thoughts and action - that affirm your belief in the universe and yourself. This is the energy that you bring to those around you.

July

Work

This month you may be involved in some competitive projects. Your dedication and skill will help you achieve success and you will be able to achieve your preferred goals. It is best to deal with internal team conflicts through discussion and open communication. Otherwise it can turn ugly. If you have been looking for a job switch, this is a good time to begin your efforts in that direction. You may also want to enrol into a professional course to up skill yourself.

Finances

Finances may be a problem this month as your payments and money is likely to get stuck in unexpected situations. It is better to be prepared for this than be caught with surprise. Avoid giving away loans or investing in futile projects as it could tie up your money and give no good returns. If you have been looking to sell your business or land, you may get good offers this month. Don't get impatient with things. Stay centred and allow the right decisions to happen.

Love

Love relationships will be fulfilling and be a source of much comfort and joy. Your relationship will need your time and effort and you will be happy doing it as well. A trip or a vacation with your loved one is likely this month. It could even be a weekend escape from the grind of everyday life. If you are looking for love, you need clarity about the kind of persona and relationship you want as well as time to invest into finding one.

Relationships

Relationships will be satisfying and bring you security and love. A father figure around you will play an important role in your life right now. Take this opportunity to learn from them and channel your passions and energy constructively in a useful direction. Friends will provide good distraction. Get-togethers with friends and even a leisure trip with them are on the cards.

Health

Health this month will be good and help you stretch yourself physically and mentally in achieving your goals. There may be times when you might indulge in excessive food and drinks which can be harmful later. Be aware and conscious of your consumption. If you have been dealing with an illness, this month can bring good results for you in that aspect.

Spirituality

You may feel a bit lost in your spiritual journey this month or perhaps just a bit confused as to how to proceed and the best path ahead for you. This is the time for you to choose what really matters to you deep within. Don't focus on the fancy stuff. At the end of the day, the fancy stuff is just a distraction, what matters is your soul's evolution.

August

Work

This month you will be focussed, confident and motivated about your work. You know you are capable and this is the right time to ask for what you are due. Your skills of dealing with people will come in handy this month as you will need to socialise and network to expand your reach, bring more work or for better opportunities. You may be tempted to solely rely on your talent, but remember, you also need to be visible to those in need of your skills.

Finances

Financially this will be a good month as you are full of good ideas and are prepared to do your work too. Your capabilities will help you become more financially secure. You may have to juggle between your job and your passion this month. Getting a second job or a freelancing project will be a good use of your time and capabilities. This is not the time to splurge your income, rather save it in sound investments.

Love

If you are in a steady relationship, you may feel dominated or feel a sense of loss of control. This can make you try to regain your control in ways that can be detrimental to your relationship. Remember, relationships are a complex mechanism of mutual sharing. If you feel insecure, it can create a ripple effect that can cause destruction. This is a good time to talk to your partner about such feelings as they can be sorted out. Chances are they are more in your perspective rather than in reality.

Relationships

You may want to reach out to old friends and family members this month, someone you had lost touch with for one reason or another. It's a good initiative on your behalf but don't expect people to behave the way they used to or how you expected. People change and evolve, sometimes we may like it, other times, we may not. But it is their journey, not yours. This is also a good time to take a good hard look at who deserves your time and attention and focus on those people.

Health

Health will be good overall. You may experience some health problems with your gut which can be irritatingly persistent. It is better to not ignore it and deal with it as soon as you can. You may have to look into not just the physical aspect of it, but the emotional and spiritual meaning and reasons too. This is a good time to invest in an energy healing journey either through receiving or learning for yourself.

Spirituality

Spiritually, this month may see a continuation of the momentum from the previous month. Often we try to find solutions to deal with the problems. But sometimes, the problem is more in the mind than out there. If difficult feelings persist, become aware of them and allow them to be felt instead of running away or distracting yourself. You are completely safe as your guardian angel watches over you.

September

Work

This month you may reach out to people or organisations for work opportunities or projects. You will be involved in quite a bit of networking. If you are looking to be an entrepreneur, working with a partner may be a good idea. However, there may be some snags and problems which can cause your work to be delayed significantly. Be prepared for this or any other such emergency situations. People around you will be willing to support you.

Finances

Financially this may be a difficult month as your expenses could easily outgrow your income causing you to struggle with some aspects. Money that was supposed to come back can get stuck further aggravating your problems. This is not the time to be choosy about your projects or assignments, rather take them in your stride. This is just a temporary phase and you will easily be able to come through it.

Love

In matters of love, this seems to be a good month. You will receive many good proposals and offers that can be taken seriously. If you are looking to just date, you will find the right people whose company you will enjoy. For those in steady relationships, this is a good time to connect to your social circle as well and be part of get-togethers as this is also a way of bonding with each other.

Relationships

While some relationships can lead you to be disappointed and sad, there are those that can uplift you and bring much light and joy in your life. This month is about focussing on what you want and spending time with those people who are your true well-wishers. A young one around you may need your mentoring and guidance. This month you will be interacting with children and that will be an enjoyable experience for you.

Health

Health will need attention and care this month. You may experience illness of a seasonal nature which can cause you to feel down and low. If you are working towards recovering from an illness, the results may not be what you have been expecting. It is time to work in tandem with your doctor. It is not your doctor that needs to be changed but your perspective towards your health. When in doubt, look within.

Spirituality

This is a good month to connect with your deity. You may choose to take the journey to them either physically by visiting their space or ethereally through experiencing their blessings and miracles. Set up an altar this month that will be your anchor for an elevated and calm spiritual state. Light a candle, offer holy water or charged water and spend some time meditating in this space everyday.

October

Work

The work flow this month will be good and is likely to keep you very busy. There may be some delays but none that can cause much problems. Social networking may keep you busy this month so you will need to prioritise your time and efforts effectively. This is a good time to chart future course of action and build a better blueprint for how you want your career or business to shape up in the near future. Your focus will help you in your efforts.

Finances

Financially this month will be comfortable overall. There may be some problems with the debtors and money matters. It is advisable to not engage in any conflicts at this time as it could blow up in your face. Keep your attention on doing your job and focus on your issues. This is not the time to meddle in someone's affairs or help them out as it can be troublesome for you.

Love

This month you will need to be practical in matters of the heart. Proposals and offers are going to be aplenty. How you go about choosing is something that will need more logic and long term thinking than something superficial. If you are looking for love or you are in a steady relationship, patience will be a virtue as the results can take time. If there is a conflict going on, give some space and take some time dealing with it rather than trying to sort it there and then.

Relationships

Relationships will be good overall. You have been delaying a decision in your life related to a relationship - it could be friends or family. This is the time to make that decision and move on with your life. Good things are coming your way in terms of people and connections. You will receive love and support from those who really matter. You will have to drop the expectation that a toxic relationship can get better with time. It won't, so it is better to decide and move on.

Health

Health will be good this month. Your persistence and good care will help you achieve the desired results in your fitness levels as well as in any recovery from illness. Sometimes, all it takes is a strong will to get better and healthier. That's what is on your side right now. Make full use of it to set any fitness plans in motion, look after your health and take steps towards healing any chronic illness.

Spirituality

Your spiritual practices have helped you achieve more stability and awareness about your mind and your environment. This is the time to go out and connect with more people. If you have been contemplating starting a business based on energy healing and divination, then this is a good time as you are being guided by higher forces. Take some time out this month to help people as they reach out to you.

November

Work

You are likely to be in a comfortable position regarding work this month. You may find yourself in a secure position at work, with support from peers and superiors. A promotion or a salary hike is on the cards. If you have been looking for a change of job, then this is a good time as you are likely to receive an exciting offer. The change would be good and will help in your career growth. Overall, this is a time to look ahead with contentment in your heart.

Finances

Your financial situation seems to be undergoing a pleasant shift. It is moving from effort to effortlessness as you open up to the opportunities that the universe brings to you and all the abundance that surrounds you. This is also a birthday month and hence a good time to celebrate the abundance in your life. Things will seem to fall together in place this month as you let go of worries. Planning for the future is still needed and needs to be done asap.

Love

In matters of love, this month may not be the best one. You may have to face some disappointments, even betrayal. This is the time to learn to distinguish between attraction and connection. Attraction is just physical, whereas connection goes deeper than that. This is also a time when you will be reminded to work on releasing toxic people and patterns in your life so that you can attract healthier relationships. You may need to work with a therapist or a coach or even with your awareness to deal with this.

Relationships

Relationships this month are going to be like walking on a tightrope. You are going to bond well with someone around you and it will be a strong support system for you. But you will also be learning how to discern logic from emotions and when you are helping someone versus when you are enabling them. Someone close to you will need your help in overcoming an emotional health issue.

Health

Health will be better this month. You will need to introduce more activity in your lifestyle for both fitness levels as well as recovering from an illness. The steps you are taking are good for you and they are working for you. It is time to take your healing journey to the next level, it could mean consulting a dietician or a personal trainer or even a coach to help you release mental blocks for manifesting better lifestyle and health.

Spirituality

This month will be about honouring your body and being kind to yourself in a way that's healthy. Your mental faculties are sharp and your intuition is at an all time high. It is the perfect time to start new projects, access new ideas and give birth to new conditions. Manifest the kind of life that you want for yourself.

December

Work

This month you may be pressed for more time as more and more work comes to you. You may be flooded with projects and ventures and you may have to pick and choose as to where you need to give your energy. Your social skills will come in handy as you will be socialising as well as diffusing conflicts with your wit and charm. If you have been waiting for the right time to pursue your passion as your profession, this is a sign for you to do that.

Finances

Finances will be average this month as you struggle to manage the inflow of money and the expenses. Things can get out of hand, so be careful with your spending habits. Avoid any major investments this month. Wait for a more opportune time. You may have to make some efforts to get the money back that you had loaned to people. This is the time to close those chapters and choose not to lend money to those who won't pay you back.

Love

This is a good month in matters of the heart. You are ready to take the journey into the realm of relationships and as you are ready, offers and proposals are also likely to come. You will need to be a bit more practical this time when choosing partners as it can help you create a more meaningful relationship or a connection. If you are in a steady relationship, it is likely to be good overall. There will be peace and love.

Relationships

It is time to close some chapters with certain people in your life. You may have given them the benefit of doubt earlier but it is time you begin to prioritise yourself over others. You may feel let down by a family member or a close friend. Instead of trying to make things better, you need to let go and find better people who deserve your care and love.

Health

This month is average in terms of health. If you have been working on recovering from a long illness, the results may not be what you had expected. You may need to change course or rethink the whole treatment plan. This is the time to create healthier goals for fitness and start working towards them. An active lifestyle will benefit you.

Spirituality

This is the end of the year as well as the end of a phase of life. The old must be released so that the new can enter. This month will be about learning attachments and detachments. You are connected to a higher source and are being guided on how to go through the difficult relationships and how to let them go, not physically but emotionally and mentally.

CHAPTER TEN

Sagittarius

November 22–December 21

Overview

2023 is a year for personal growth. Even though life externally will feel perfect and that everything is in order, yet inside you may feel as if something is missing or incomplete. You will be compelled to take the journey inwards as it will provide you the missing pieces of your spirituality.

This year you may find yourself connecting to people from your past or perhaps even being nostalgic about them. Personally though you are likely to be more grounded and this will help you deal with many life situations and relationships with ease. You have the wisdom to know your boundaries, the only challenge sometimes is remembering to assert them.

Professionally this year will be fruitful and you are not likely to get any chance to think or take in all that happens. It will be fast paced and there could be a lot of travel involved too. You may get tangled in some conflicts which will be purely due to inflated egos and insecurities. Your best chance at dealing with these is to feel secure about yourself and refuse to participate in such dramas.

You are likely to question your abilities this year and there will be periods when you begin to question your worth. This can cause you to feel not good enough and can spiral a lot of emotions and situations out of control. Working with a coach or an emotional therapist is highly recommended to help you deal with your shadow self.

Motivation levels will be high as well as your energy levels. On one hand this will help you achieve many goals this year personally and professionally, but on the down side, it is also likely to make you more anxious and angry if you do not learn to channel all your energy constructively. It will be advisable to keep your tempers in check this year or it can land you in trouble.

In your personal life, you are likely to be a strong support system for those around you and people will be able to count on you in times of need. But this can also make you exhausted and drained from so much social contact. Take some time out every now and then to destress and gather your energies. Trips to a retreat will be good for you.

First half of the year will be mostly about family and connecting to loved ones. You also like to connect with your professional colleagues in that manner but it is not always the best thing always. You will need to learn, remember and assert your boundaries in life if you want less drama. Second half of the year will be about learning and training. You are likely to attend training seminars and workshops that can help you professionally and personally. This is a good year to invest in further education or learning a new skill.

January

Work

Work will be good as new opportunities come to you in abundance this month. You are likely to be recommended by your superiors in a good light and that will give a boost to your career and position. But at the same time it is also likely to increase your workload and pressure to perform which can be daunting at times. Though you will be able to manage your work and also create some sense of balance in your life, it will still be taxing on your nerves. So take extra caution against bad health.

Finances

Finances will be average. Even though money is flowing in, yet the expenses also keep mounting creating the imbalance. You will need to watch your spending habits month if you want to meet your financial goals this month. A side job or a new project can bring in added income which is likely to provide you some relief. But the money can get delayed. If you have applied for any loans, they may not get approved in time.

Love

In matters of love, this month is likely to be busy. If you are single, you may go on a dating spree until you find the right one. Be confident of your strengths and don't compromise. If you are in a steady relationship, there will be happy times with your partner. You are also likely to get involved with your partner in a professional matter and enjoy the association even though it will have its own problems related to egos clashes.

Relationships

Relationships are likely to be peaceful and happy. You may get to spend time with a family member and the company is likely to be surprisingly enjoyable. You will mostly like to keep to yourself and enjoy your solitude this month. There is also a possibility of you taking solo trips. In all of this, remember to communicate this to those who care about you so that they don't take it personally.

Health

Health will need attention and care as there could be something that can trouble you enough to need doctor's help. Don't avoid any minor symptoms. You could experience problems related to lowered immunity like cold and flu, or a health issue related to water imbalance in the body. A mix of modern medicine and alternative healing will be helpful. This is also a reminder to spend time caring for yourself in your self-love journey.

Spirituality

You cannot always keep giving. You must be able to receive as well, otherwise an imbalance is created not just in the universe but also within you. You will need to look into how you really feel and deal with it. You will have to deal with it sooner or later. The longer you delay. The more difficult it is likely to be. Allow others to help you, reach out for support. Don't let your ego block you from receiving. It is only when you receive, can you give effectively.

February

Work

Work is likely to be slow this month as some projects are completed, others appear to have hit a snag. There may be some delays, but none that will disrupt your schedules. This is the time to take a step back and have a look at the big picture before the next step. There is much to look forward to. This is just a pause before something good comes your way. You will receive the long awaited results of a project or work you have done. The results are likely to be in line with your efforts.

Finances

Finances can be erratic this month. You will need to be constantly on the lookout for opportunities if you are an entrepreneur and want regular inflow of funds. There may be some impulsive decisions about spending which can set you back and throw your budget off track. But a little bit of care and caution can save you from that. New sources of income are likely to open up this month as your efforts bear fruits in that direction.

Love

If you are looking for love, there is a possibility that you may find yourself trying to make sense of people you meet. It can be confusing and difficult to gauge their true intentions. This is the time to cut through the drama and sweet talk and notice any red flags. If someone looks too good to be true, they probably are. Keep your guards up and avoid revealing yourself completely until you know for sure. This is also a month when some of your toxic relationship patterns may come to light and you will be compelled to look into and deal with them for good.

Relationships

You may indulge in some monetary transactions in your relationships this month. Remember not to just give your money away but to make sure it's actually helping them or not. You will need to create stronger boundaries around certain people so that they can neither take advantage of you nor disturb your peace of mind with their thoughts and words. Friends will be a source of comfort and joy. Get-togethers with friends are on the cards.

Health

Health will be average this month. You will need to be consistent with your efforts for your health and fitness levels if you wish to achieve the results you want. You are on the right path and your ideas are good. The progress is likely to be slow but sure. Keep yourself optimistic and focus on your efforts one day at a time.

Spirituality

This month is about looking forward more than looking behind in the past. You cannot change what happened, at the most you can process it and heal it so it doesn't affect your present. But the real point of effect and meaning is in the now. That is where you need to focus. This is also the time to deal with any guilt or lack of forgiveness from your past that is not letting you move ahead peacefully.

March

Work

The pace of work will be average. You may struggle to deal with some clients or peers this month. Keep a check on your temper and stay calm during any negotiations. A new project or a job offer this month can get you into top gear. This is an important time to strike a balance between your personal and professional life. It would be good to take care of who you share your crucial details and information with as it could be misused.

Finances

Financially you may feel stuck this month. Although the income will match your expenses, yet the inability to have surplus can make you feel stressed and worried. You may have invested funds which are unlikely to give you the kind of returns that you had expected. It is better to learn from the experience and only invest in standard schemes. A new financial opportunity may come your way. Do consider it seriously.

Love

This month will be very productive in terms of love matters. For those looking for love, this is a good time to start exploring portals or social groups in search of a suitable partner or date. For those in steady relationships, this month will bring much joy and companionship with your partner. You may plan to take your relationship to the next level. There will be understanding and you will be involved in either house hunting or home decoration with them.

Relationships

This month you may want to connect with someone from the past in hope of re-living the happy moments. Meeting an elder or a grandparent can bring back the joyful memories from childhood. You may experience some resistance from certain people close to you - friends or family. You need to stick to your ideas and you don't have to change yourself to be accepted by anyone. This may make you feel left out but it also means space has been created in your life to attract those who can appreciate you for who you are.

Health

Health is likely to be good. But your worries about your health can complicate things. Often it is not the physical health issue, but the worry and fear that makes it difficult to recover. If you are recovering from a chronic illness, you will need more rest to recuperate. Otherwise health will support you in your endeavours. You are likely to indulge yourself in the company of friends and family. So you will need to be watchful of that.

Spirituality

Sometimes, escaping the problem is not the solution. Often fear is in the mind and it turns little problems into huge mountains. You are stronger than you think you are. You have the strength to deal with anything that life throws at you and come out with a happy outcome. This will be a good time to work on your shadow aspects - those parts of you that you consider ugly or unacceptable.

April

Work

Work will be busy this month as more of it flows in than you can handle. There is likely to be progress on many projects. Working with a team of peers will accelerate the pace of your work. There is also a need to be careful this month about any office politics going on around you as you could potentially become a target of it. Keep your eyes and ears open. Re-evaluate the people that you trust in your professional life.

Finances

Financially this month is going to be a mixed bag. Even though your financial situation remains secure, you may receive a major blow from a financial deal that breaks down or an investment that results in a loss. This is not the time to take risks. You need to be cautious as there is likely to be a lot of unpredictability in financial matters. As a business, you may have to dip into your reserve funds until the situation gets better.

Love

If you are looking for love, this month will be good for you as you are likely to meet someone who shares many similarities with you and you hit it off instantly. However, before taking it seriously, give this some time. If you are in a steady relationship, this month you may experience conflicts and strains in your relationships mostly due to miscommunications and misunderstandings. This is the time to clear doubts and open channels of communication.

Relationships

This month you are likely to want to spend time only with those closest to you. You can be quite protective about them. But this can sometimes lead them to feel suffocated. You may want to loosen the hold and allow them to reach out to you as well. This is not the best time to pick up quarrels or grudges with someone around you as no matter who wins, both sides will end up losing this ego battle. Forgive and move on.

Health

Health will be good this month. You are in a good place to begin a fitness routine that will help you with more flexibility and calmness. Activities like yoga, tai chi etc. will be very helpful. Avoid any strenuous activity to begin with. Build your strength gradually. You have the right ideas for your healing and health journey. You just need to put them to practise.

Spirituality

This month you may feel tempted by short term gains from your spiritual practices, but this is a reminder for you to focus on the practice instead of what it is giving you. Any activity you do will bring results inevitably. But if you get distracted by the results and pursue those practices for the rewards, you are likely to miss out on many things that come along with it. Don't push yourself too much this month, take it easy and focus on things one at a time.

May

Work

This is the month of making plans and being very thorough with their execution. You may have to face some unexpected hurdles and delays at work. You will need to have strategies to bypass them so they don't affect your progress. Someone at the workplace may be withholding some information which can help you create better plans. You will have to be to the point in your meetings and negotiations which can go in your favour.

Finances

Finances will be good this month. You may receive money from unexpected sources that will help you. This is a good time to invest in further education in a field of your choosing. It could be to upgrade your skills, or learn a new skill set. You are in the right mindset for that. There may be some difficulties regarding payments this month but a little effort will resolve them.

Love

This month can be a bit disappointing in matters of love. If there is someone you had been looking forward to or been pursuing in hopes of a proposal, it may not turn out the way you expected. If you are in a steady relationship, you may feel somewhat left out by your partner as they get busy with their work. But remember, this is not about you. You will have to deal with your own insecurities and look at the bright side of the situation rather than taking it personally. Things are not as bad as you may think.

Relationships

You will have to be quick about your decisions. Reach out to those who matter to you often. You don't have to wait for them to connect with you. You may feel sad about a friend moving away this month. But this is also a time of endings and new beginnings for you. As the old leaves, the new arrives. Make an effort to go out and meet new people. You are ready for this. Just meet new people with an expectation of getting to know them and nothing more.

Health

Health this month can be somewhat delicate. You will need plenty of rest and alone time to recuperate and gather your energies. You may experience aches and pains in the body, they could be due to elevated heat levels in the body. If the pain persists, get it checked with a doctor. Some form of mild activity will be beneficial. Nature and the mountain side will have healing benefits for you.

Spirituality

You may find yourself worrying too much this month over matters that are not in your control. You may want to learn that life is not about controlling and there will be times when things will not go the way we want them to. This month will be about learning to trust the universe and surrender to a higher power knowing that the situation will be handled in a fair and just manner. Even if the trust is mechanical to begin with, practice affirmations like "The universe has my back" or "I am being cared for in every way."

June

Work

This month you are likely to be overburdened with work as you take on more than you can handle. This is time to learn to delegate as there are people available around you to help you out with this. You do not have to do this alone. Opportunities will be abundant this month but making decisions may prove to be difficult as you could experience confusion due to lack of relevant information and time.

Finances

Finances will be good as you will be more restrained in your spending habits this month. Money inflow is likely to improve as new sources of income open up to you. This is the time to be optimistic but not rash. Someone around you is likely to be wasteful with the money which can prove to be difficult for you to control. You will have to be watchful about any expenditures that happen from your funds.

Love

In matters of love, this looks like a good month. If marriage is on your mind, it is likely to materialise soon. Your efforts at finding a suitable partner will be fruitful. Don't compromise on your basic values. For those in a steady relationship, this is the time to build a deeper connection with your partner. You will be able to spend good quality time with them.

Relationships

You will be looking deeper into your relationship patterns as this month you may feel the need to shift them for the better. Those who are toxic - friends or family - you will want to create distance from them so that people who really are your well-wishers and are capable of having a healthy relationship can come close to you. This may prove to be more difficult than you imagined but deep down you know it's for your best.

Health

Health will be good. But you also know you need to be more strict with your lifestyle, food and activity, especially if you are dealing with a lifestyle disorder like blood pressure and diabetes. You will be able to handle your cravings and health consequently. Your family and loved ones will be supportive in your health journey in every way.

Spirituality

You may experience yourself being more worried and stressed over little things this month. It doesn't mean there is something wrong with you. It just means that you are becoming increasingly sensitive to your environment which is a sign of spiritual evolution. It is time to avoid harsh relationships, situations, environments and chemicals. Instead of worrying, focus your thoughts and feelings on only your goal and you will make your mark.

July

Work

Progress on the work front may be slow this month. You may have to abandon or delay a few projects because of viability issues. If you are on the verge of choosing a new field or career, this is perhaps not the best time. Stick to what you are doing at present and delay your decision until you have more clarity about it. You may be tempted to take up a job offer which promises more. But it would be wise to look into it in detail before going ahead with it.

Finances

Finances will be good but will need close supervision and a tight rein otherwise the expenses can throw your plans into jeopardy. If investing in a business, make sure to thoroughly check for its viability as well as suitability for you. This is not the time to make risky decisions about finances. Better times are coming soon, safe investments without lock-in periods would be a better option.

Love

You will need to use your head more than your heart in matters of love this month. If you are looking for love, finding the right person may not happen soon enough this month. But meanwhile, it is better to stay single than associate with someone who can have ulterior motives or even a toxic narcissist. If you are in a steady relationship and there are issues that haven't been addressed openly, this is the time to do it before it affects your relationship negatively.

Relationships

Your judgement about people is right and you need to follow your instincts. This month it will help you immensely as you try to navigate the landscape of difficult relationships. You may not be able to create distance between you and them so you will have to learn to deal with them at close quarters. You are likely to be supported by an authority figure in your life who will also be able to guide you through this.

Health

Health will be good overall this month. You may experience some distress with your digestive system and complaints related to the liver. Cards indicate this is a good time to detox and watch your food habits closely. Fasting once a week and eating according to your Ayurvedic body constitution will do you a lot of good.

Spirituality

You have a lot of love within you to share with the world. But that doesn't mean you keep pouring it over people who don't value it. When you do that, you are actually not valuing yourself and your love. This month, you will need to learn more about self-love and explore this concept practically and not just theoretically. You can start with doing things for yourself that you would do for someone who you love.

August

Work

Work this month will be good. You have plenty of opportunities flowing to you. This is also a good time to consider expansion for your business or franchise. A work related trip abroad could materialise this month. If you have been looking for a job change or a better offer, you are likely to receive one this month. You will have to be very particular about the fine print if you are signing any major deals this month. It is better to be safe than sorry.

Finances

Finances will be good and will support your projects and any expenses that may come up this month. You will move away from your financial troubles soon. This is a time to be hopeful and optimistic about your financial future. You will be able to undertake any projects or ventures that were stuck due to financial issues in the past.

Love

In matters of love, this month is likely to be a mixed bag with some good and some not so good things. You may experience some disappointment in matters of the heart but you will be able to move on pretty quickly and look for someone who resonates with you better. In your steady relationship, you will have to work hard and make an effort to show your love through acts of love. It will be good to understand your partner's love language and express your love in their language.

Relationships

Relationships will bring you much joy and happiness this year as you get to spend good quality time with your loved ones and extended family. A celebration in the family is on the cards as well as an addition to the family. If you have been considering doing business with a family member, this is a good time to think about it seriously. Remember to make it official and have the deal in black and white instead of just words.

Health

Health will be good this month. Your efforts that you have been making consistently will be rewarded. If you haven't done anything dedicatedly, this is the time to begin. Your health is directly correlated to your efforts that you make for your health and fitness. Laziness can be your energy this month as it can produce more inertia making it difficult for you to begin making the changes in your lifestyle.

Spirituality

Sagittarians are known for their extremes. And this month it will be visible as you swing between the extremes of pessimism and blind optimism. It is healthier to see the big picture and be realistic about yourself and your goals. Journalling will be of great help as it will help you see the truth of the situation clearly. As you learn to balance your perspective, you will notice the external world around you also comes into harmony.

September

Work

Work this month will be good. Your creative ideas will find recognition and you will be able to implement them with support from all quarters. This is also a good time to look for a study program to enhance or upgrade your skills. A managerial program could be the next step for you. For those looking to expand their businesses, this month will be favourable. Good news from overseas will bring plenty of opportunities.

Finances

Finances will be average. You will be able to meet your needs and expenses without much problem. You may end up spending money and time on or with someone that you may regret later. So awareness about it will help you not regret your actions. The money that you had given to help someone as a loan is not likely to come back this month making things a bit difficult for you not just financially but also with the concerned person.

Love

In matters of love, this month will be favourable. If you are seeking love, you are likely to receive good proposals from suitable suitors. Don't be afraid to reach out to the one who you are interested in. If you are in a steady relationship, this month will be a mixed bag. Things can be difficult at times with differences of opinions and it can lead to a breakdown in communication. However, you just need to be open enough to allow clear communication to resolve any issues with ease.

Relationships

Relationships for you overall are going through a change. This month too you are likely to see the changes as well in many dynamics of close relations. This is not the time to take any action or do something proactively. Allow the things to unfold and whatever is needed of you in the moment, just do that. You don't have to go out of your way to please people anymore. There are plenty of people who love and care for you. Focus on them.

Health

Health will be average as you struggle with some seasonal changes and problems. You may experience some issues with skin, hair and immunity. Focus on having a nutritious diet as it can go a long way in ensuring good health. Seek a wise doctor's counsel to help ease your recovery. Timely steps taken for your health will be important this month.

Spirituality

When faced with matters of making decisions this month, it is important for you to keep in mind that those decisions should come from a place of compassion for yourself. It is time to release judgments about yourself and others and focus on the love and light that is within everyone.

October

Work

Work will be busy and abundant this month. You will need to be judicious with your resources so that you don't stretch yourself too thin. New job offers can be tempting and worth having a look into. You will need to be very practical in professional matters this month as it will help you stay focussed and impartial. Stay away from being complacent. This is not the time to let opportunities slip by.

Finances

Financially this month will be above average. Inflow of funds and working capital will keep you going. You will also be able to stick to your budget and make the savings that you had intended. However, there can be some unpredictability regarding money in the near future. So this is a good time to take care and precautions. Do not spend blindly. Being a little miser will be good for your finances this month.

Love

In matters of love, this month will be fruitful. If you are in search of your soulmate, you are likely to meet yours this month in the most unexpected of places. So make sure you put your best foot forward whenever stepping out of the house. For the ones in a steady relationship or marriage, this month will bring opportunities to spend time with your loved ones as well as the extended family or friends. You will experience much joy and fun with your loved one.

Relationships

Relationships will be happy and a source of joy for you. You will find your interactions with young members or children very enjoyable. You will be able to mentor or guide them as well, especially as they enter adulthood. You may enrol in a course with a family member or a friend which will help you learn a new skill and also create more bonding between you and them. Some of the relationships in your life are going through a period of change which will unravel in the next few months.

Health

Health will be average this month. A health issue from the past can trouble you, so taking caution and preventive measures will be helpful. You may have been planning to get into a new health program or an exercise routine but it may not happen this month despite your best efforts. It is better to start small, something you can do without much resistance just to get started and then pick up pace. Vata related issues can trouble you this month. Using spices like dry ginger and ginseng will be helpful.

Spirituality

What inspires you? What is it that wakes you up and motivates you to get out of bed? That thought, idea is a part of your purpose. Remember it and follow it. It is your guiding star. Anytime you feel a lack of inspiration in life or as if there is nothing left to live for, look for that idea or thought. It will lead you, guide you to your destiny.

November

Work

Work will be good this month. You are in the right place to ask for what you deserve. If you have been waiting for a better opportunity, it is time to go look for it rather than waiting for it to show up on its own. If you are trying to handle two jobs or fields of work, this month it would be easier as you would be able to give your best to both. But soon you will have to figure out the one which interests you more and is better for your future and focus on it.

Finances

Finances are likely to be unpredictable this month. It is possible for money to go out as soon as it comes in. So you will need to check your budget and keep tight reins on the spendings. If you are looking for investments for a business, you are likely to find it in your inner circle of friends or family. A reward from a past investment can bring in joy for you and your family. Inheritance matters are likely to go smoothly this month.

Love

In matters of love, this month is likely to bring you joy and success. If you are looking for love, you will need to use both your head and heart. Don't jump into any commitments too soon, but if you have been thinking about it for some time with your partner, this is the right time to go ahead with it. If you are in a steady relationship or marriage, you will need to be a source of emotional stability and practical guidance for your partner this month.

Relationships

Relationships will bring joy as quite a few new changes are happening. An addition to the family is on the cards. Your relations with certain people from your past are healing. It is time to forgive and heal what happened and look ahead towards better times. An event that you have been waiting for a long time is likely to happen soon in your family. Children will bring happiness to you and you are likely to spend good time with them.

Health

Health will be good. Your efforts towards improving your health are helping you reach closer to your health goals. However the progress may seem slow this month. But don't let this discourage you. It is time to keep going and continuing your efforts. If you have been working towards recovery from an illness, this is a favourable time for that. Pay attention towards lower immunity levels and keep working to improve them.

Spirituality

Procrastination can hinder you from moving towards the life you want. And usually procrastination is just fears showing up in different ways and voices. It is time to keep your attention focussed on your goal and work towards it. Anytime you feel you are not good enough or it's too huge for you, remember, help is always available and most often the fears are just fears, they have no truth.

December

Work

Work will be good this month. You are likely to get recognition for your job and a commensurate reward. You are also likely to receive good offers for jobs from competitors which can become somewhat difficult to choose from. You will be able to maintain a work-life balance this month. If you have been looking for a change of job or career, this is the time to take a good hard look at what you have and where you want to be. You may have to take a leap of faith in this scenario.

Finances

Finances will be good. You are likely to receive an additional source of income this month which will help you take care of any additional expenses. If you have been looking for investment opportunities, you may have to spend some time researching good ones. It is better not to go with what anyone suggests but really do your research and speak to experts about it. Any loans or investments you have been looking for for your business or venture, you are likely to receive them this month.

Love

In matters of love this month is likely to be a little challenging as you try to deal with ego battles and conflicts. It is imperative to remember that you and your partner are not opposites but part of the same team. As long as you remember this, you will be able to sail through disagreements. If you are looking for love, you are likely to receive positive communication from someone and things will move ahead quickly.

Relationships

Relationships will keep you busy as someone could come calling from overseas or far away and bring some good times and good news. There is a good possibility of you meeting new people this month and forge some new friendships. You may feel a certain connection with them which can feel very deep. However, it is recommended that you do not delve too deep to begin with and let it grow over time. A young one in the family is ready to embark on their higher education journey.

Health

Health will be good overall. Any efforts that you may have been making have borne fruits. This is also a time to reconsider any new plans of action or a new way of approaching your health goals now. If you have been dealing with a major illness or accidents, the worst is behind you. It may take some time to recover completely, but it is important to take little steps everyday.

Spirituality

The universe operates on the principle of energy exchange. It is important to remember that you are also completing the exchange. This month, remember to complete your debts, whether monetary or energetic. Also it is important to be careful about where you spend your time and energy as it is a valuable resource and it determines your state of mind as well. But once you have invested your time in something, don't second guess yourself.

Capricorn

December 22–January 19

Overview

2023 is going to be a year of ease and new opportunities. There is going to be a certain ease in your life which can manifest itself in personal as well as professional areas of life. This year the focus will be on family, relationships and personal satisfaction.

A new wave of energy in your life brings new people and new situations which will prompt you to learn skills that will help you in dealing with this new energy. Family life will be overall satisfying and bring much joy.

Celebrations in the family and with close loved ones is likely to be the feature of the year.

Fresh opportunities at the workplace are likely to bring a renewed sense of enthusiasm and optimism. For those looking at the start of a career, this year present many good opportunities and ideas. But it will take a lot of effort and an openness to learning to get comfortable with your work. This is a good year to turn your passion into profession as your energy and situations around you align making the process effortless.

Professionally, the year will bring good opportunities and also give you the chance to get more stability in your workplace. People and peers are likely to be amicable. A positive work environment will help you create better work-life balance. Job opportunities abroad are likely to come your way. So if you have been looking for this, 2023 is likely to be lucky for you.

Personally, you will need to be more practical along with emotional as you navigate the landscape of relationships. People around you look forward to speaking to you as you can provide them a calm space and a listening ear. Emotionally this year could be a roller coaster and you may find yourself looping in certain thought processes. Grounding yourself will be immensely helpful.

First half of the year may bring a few hurdles and you may experience lack of energy or motivation to get things done. You will need to be kind to yourself and allow life to take its course. Remember sometimes life pulls you back only to propel you forward with much greater speed. Second half of the year will bring much appreciation and recognition in many areas of life. A sense of fulfilment will be there. Many tasks or projects that had been ongoing or on hold, will come to a good close soon.

January

Work

Professionally, this month is likely to give average results. You may be faced with difficult choices at work or even in your career which will define your professional life for some years to come. A little soul searching will make the choice much easier and help lead you to a more fulfilling career and profession. Communication will be swift and open creating more opportunities for you. For those in the field of communication, this is going to be an exciting month.

Finances

Financially this can be a difficult month with many delays and some stress. You may feel burdened under the increasing finances. There will be a need to carefully watch your expenses and avoid extravagant spendings this month. A moderate approach to buying and a minimalist attitude will be helpful. Fundings may take some time to arrive. Instead of worrying about it too much, it is better to look at other aspects of business for now.

Love

If you are looking for love, you are likely to meet some new and interesting prospects this month. It is important to have an open mind and a light hearted approach to the whole process instead of getting bogged down by making it a matter of life and death. If you are in a relationship or looking to get into one, get some clarity into what you really want from your partner and relationship along with what you bring to it. Do not run away from any problems, rather try and sort them out.

Relationships

This month may bring up old memories which are not so pleasant. You may have been still looking at fresh new relationships from the lens of what happened in an old relationship that is in the past right now. Give yourself a chance to heal your heart and to someone to help you with it. Issues related to children can cause sleepless nights and worries. Most of the worries are just in the mind. Instead of stressing about things, focus on what you can do about it.

Health

This is likely to be an important month in matters related to health. If you have been struggling with an illness or the recovery has been very slow, you are likely to meet a health professional or doctor who will guide you in a manner which will make the healing process simpler and faster. Don't be afraid to seek out help and even second opinions. Weather related issues can be troublesome this month.

Spirituality

This month you may feel as if god or the universe is not listening to you and you are feeling left out. But it is not the case. Sometimes what is needed is an intent to receive help and ask for it. This month affirmations will be helpful. Any ego related issues around asking for help are likely to come to the fore. Remember, you don't become small just because you are asking or receiving help. It is part of the exchange process which has to complete itself.

February

Work

You may be tempted to take quick and swift action this month at your workplace. But it might lead to problems later on. So it is suggested that you take it slow and follow a balanced approach instead of an extreme one. Opportunities for work and business will be plenty. This is a good time to plan ahead and make space for more work and life as well. You will be able to make better decisions and implement them as well.

Finances

Finances this month can be somewhat troubling as you struggle to deal with some unexpected expenses. Though the opportunities for income are likely to increase, they may take time to fructify. You may have to deal with some losses in one of your investments. It is not advisable to invest too much in one avenue. There is likely to be some major change in how you handle finances. It will be prudent to save for times when you may need the extra liquidity.

Love

You may be wearing your heart on your sleeve this month as you could likely meet some interesting people. But don't be too quick to get into any relationships as it may not be exactly what you are looking for. It is possible for you to get distracted with surface things such as looks or find yourself getting striated to someone just because they are giving attention to you. It is important this month to stand your ground and do not compromise on your base values.

Relationships

Relationships can be somewhat confusing this month as you try to make sense of things and intentions of others. This is the time to understand your priorities and do not compromise on them. Finding time for family members and loved ones can be difficult this month. If you have been planning to start a business or a venture with a friend or family member, it is better to really look into the viability of it as well as the equation between the two of you.

Health

Health will need your attention as you may have to deal with some issues which may take some time and effort to diagnose. Do not ignore anything minor too and work towards healing it this month. It will be better to look at the health situation from a very practical point of view instead of thinking about it emotionally. It is time to get the annual health checkup, especially if you have been postponing it for some time now.

Spirituality

There needs to be a balanced give and take in any area of your life including relationships. Any imbalance in any aspect, whether giving or receiving, can make things unbalanced and create karmic problems in the future. Doing some form of charity this month will be beneficial. This month is also a reminder that not everything has to be transactional, for example, unconditional love. If it is an alien concept for you, it is time to explore it for yourself.

March

Work

Work this month will be good as your efforts are seen and rewarded. Keep up with your efforts and focus on your job instead of on politics and gossip. You are under assessment favourably and it is your dedication and quality of work that will help you rise through your career. You may also find yourself connecting with your old network of peers which is likely to be a pleasant experience.

Finances

Financially things are looking up this month. As new sources of income bring that additional inflow, things become a little easy. Your financial decisions need to be grounded in practical decisions and vision for the future. It is time to take a moment to gain a bird's eye view of your present financial situation and set up goals of what you want for the future. You will be able to save some money this month.

Love

This can be a difficult month in terms of love and close relationships. You can end up feeling as if you are carrying the burden of the relationship and feel betrayed as the other person doesn't seem to be contributing much to it. It is time to reevaluate the connection and check if one of you has evolved or grown apart emotionally. A breakup doesn't have to be fraught with conflict. It can be a peaceful parting as well. On the other hand, it might mean creating space for someone with whom you are meant to take things more seriously ahead into living together or marriage.

Relationships

Relationships are likely to be pleasant overall. A family get-together is on the cards. A happy occasion could be the cause for celebration and family and friends coming together. Matters related to inheritance can also come up at this time and are likely to be settled peacefully. This is the time to break away from past influences. A young one around you is ready to embark on their independent journey.

Health

Health this month will be average. Energy levels will be better and the body will experience more vitality. You could experience some problems with your cardiovascular system and will need to pay close attention to it. Creating a healthy lifestyle and making small changes to the way you eat will go a long way towards ensuring better health. Your health will directly reflect the kind of efforts you put into it.

Spirituality

This is a time to embrace the divine feminine aspects within you. This includes qualities of nurturing, creativity, compassion and the ability to flow with the universe and life. Connect to the energy of mother earth in different ways like gardening, walking barefoot and working with sand and soil. This will be extremely grounding and bring more peace to your erratic thought processes.

April

Work

Work can be somewhat frustrating this month as you experience disappointments and delays. A project or job that you had been waiting to start can get postponed causing some problems. If you have been thinking of starting a business, this is not the best time to take action. Wait until things fall together and then move ahead with your action plan. Don't think you are stuck and can't move, take this as a prep time for action to happen soon.

Finances

Finances may get delayed this month as some payments and work can get stalled due to unexpected reasons. Keep your cool and find out alternatives to get your work done and receive the finances necessary. On the positive side, as money inflow reduces or gets delayed this month, the expenses also will likely stay under control.

Love

This is likely to be an average month in terms of love and give mixed results. Your efforts to woo your crush are likely to bear fruits. Something that you had been waiting for since some time, that proposal is likely to come your way this month. But when it comes, do not let your ego make you reject it. If you are in a steady relationship, things are likely to be smooth and happy. You will spend some good quality time with your beloved.

Relationships

If some relationships have been a source of problem and heartache, they will soon be healed or move out of your life. This month forebodes well for relationships and friendships. You are likely to meet some new interesting people who can turn into good friends eventually. Family will be supportive and help you in your growth. A family get-together especially for a celebration is on the cards.

Health

Health will be good this month. Your restraint will help you deal with many health problems. However temptations will also abound. It is a good time to begin a new exercise routine, something that suits your body as well as temperament. Explore different kinds of exercises including some oriental forms. Recovery from illness is on the cards.

Spirituality

Our actions when aligned with universal energies always bear good fruits. So if things are not happening in your timeline despite your best efforts, perhaps you will need to adapt your time to what the universe wants. This month will be about learning to trust the process and flow of the universe.

May

Work

Work this month is likely to be slow but steady. You are going to receive many opportunities which may seem tempting enough but you will need to make sure they have some substance before moving ahead with any option. It is time to make some changes and shift gears in your career. You know it is time to move ahead towards progress. The change can feel uncertain and challenging but it is required.

Finances

Finances will be average this month. Some payments may get delayed but it won't affect your work and progress as much. This is not the time to make rash decisions but sleep on them before deciding. Some loans are likely to get repaid this month bringing you much relief. Doing charity in some form this month will help you change your mindset towards money.

Love

You are likely to invest your time in finding a good partner for yourself. Self awareness and recognising your patterns will help you figure out the kind of relationship that will be best for you. If you are in a steady relationship, you need to make an effort into reigniting the passion in the relationship. Avoid temptation to find shortcuts to your happiness as it will negatively impact your existing relationship.

Relationships

Relationships this month will see some changes. It is best to take some time before making any decisions or taking any actions. Many relationships are likely to undergo some changes mostly because you are growing as a person. When you grow, people who do not resonate with you and are unwilling to grow as well tend to gradually move away from your life. It is time to introspect on the kind of people you want in your life and work towards it.

Health

Health will be average. You may experience fears about your health issues and this can lead you to feel more anxious and stressed about yourself. Stay away from self diagnosis and consult a holistic health practitioner for guidance. Spending time in nature and solitude will be healing for you.

Spirituality

This month will be about taking on new journeys and learning to adapt to change. You are grounded and centred enough to make difficult decisions on the spur of the moment. If you feel a lack of purpose in life, focus on service. How can you serve and be useful for the beings around you. Your focus on service will help you take on the new journey with a sense of adventure and optimism.

June

Work

You will need to be more focussed on your work and have more clarity about your priorities. This can be a sensitive month so you will need to be careful and pay attention to any gossip or politics going on around you at the workplace. Do not make any rash decisions or speak anything in the heat of the moment that you may have to regret later on. This is a good time to learn a new skill or up skill yourself in your field of work.

Finances

Finances will again be average. This is the month to nurture what you have and stay away from unnecessary expenditure. Money inflows may not be as expected causing you some problems. Do not invest anywhere or lend any money to someone as it is not likely to bear fruit. Seat away from specially shady investment schemes and people. Your focus about work and money needs to be laser-like. Let go of confusions and focus on what's important for you.

Love

You are likely to meet your soulmate this month. Cards are positive with regards to love and matters of the heart. If you are in a steady relationship, your connection with your partner will be renewed and you will spend good quality time with them. If your partner has been away, you are likely to receive some good communication from them. Things related to relationships are likely to move ahead positively and smoothly.

Relationships

You are likely to be quite busy this month socially as you connect with people and be a gracious host. Parties and social evenings will take up your time and be constructive as well. However this can be exhausting for you, so remember to take some time for yourself to fill your cup as well. Overseas connections are on the cards, either receiving news and visitors from abroad or reaching out to them.

Health

Health will be good and will help you meet the demands of your social life. Remember to seek out help in case you feel under the weather physically or even emotionally. Talking to a supportive coach or counsellor will have a healing effect on you. Take some time out to tend to your passion as it will revive your joy and interest. Be careful of where you spend your energies.

Spirituality

Any spiritual activity that you perform this month with discipline and regularity will be extremely beneficial for you. Some form of discipline always helps you to bring out your best. You may find yourself being a bit too stubborn about the way you want to do things generally in your life this month, just remember to look at the bigger picture while getting particular about the details as well.

July

Work

This month will be very good for work related things. Your dreams will come close to being fulfilled which will be a source of much joy and satisfaction. A promotion in rank is on the cards bringing with it monetary benefits too. You are likely to be in a leadership position and will be able to lead your team with compassion, strength and wisdom. Continuing to upgrade your skills, including soft skills, will pave the way for your growth.

Finances

Overconfidence in financial matters can lead to some problems with money and people. Stay away from making decisions which you will regret later. It is better to consult a known expert or wait for the right time to make those decisions. In matters of inheritance, you may experience a setback. But do not let it dishearten you as you have not lost all of it. Keep moving ahead without holding on to bitter experiences and stay away from indulging in any politics.

Love

In matters of the heart this month, you are likely to use more of your head instead of your heart. While this is useful especially when it comes to discerning people whether they are good or not for you, it can also hamper your increasing connections that could have been very deep and meaningful. So strike a balance between your head and your heart, look for the positive and listen to your instincts.

Relationships

Relationships this month are likely to be good and a source of joy. Marriage in the family is on the cards. A young adult around you is ready to embark on their journey and will benefit from your guidance. People in the family and friends are likely to seek your opinion and wisdom this month. Visitors from overseas will bring some good news.

Health

Health will need care. You tend to overexert yourself when feeling okay and forget to look after your health until it starts to ring major alarm bells. This month, you may experience pains in your back, legs and lower abdomen issues. It is time to focus on improving your diet and having a regular exercise regimen. Stay away from heavy fatty foods. Fasting can help, consult an expert before doing it.

Spirituality

Connecting to nature is something that brings you a lot of peace and contentment. If you haven't done that in some time, do it now. Ditch your music and earphones and listen to the sound of nature, let it heal your heart. Active meditations this month will be helpful.

August

Work

Work this month is likely to bring some disappointment. However the situation is not as bad as you may think. Chances are you may be catastrophizing too much leading to increased levels of stress and anxiety so much so that you find yourself incapable of taking any decisions. Avoid sharing your issues or thoughts and ideas with everyone except for your closest well wishers as they could either misuse it or take advantage of it.

Finances

Finances are likely to be good and stable this month. It is time to nurture what you have instead of giving it away. This is a good time to look at long term gains and investments. Any financial approvals that you have been waiting for are soon coming your way. Creative projects that you have been thinking of starting and looking for investments for that are likely to materialise this month.

Love

You are likely to meet some interesting people this month that may have the potential to be your partner. However, it is suggested that you do not take any decisions or make any commitments this month and give your connection some time to grow. Trust your first impressions but do seek to know more about the person in different situations as well. Steady relationships are going to be smooth. It is time for you and your partner to take some time alone for self introspection.

Relationships

This month is likely to be about marriages, connections, partnerships and meeting new people who become a part of your life. If you have been looking to adopt a child, this month you are likely to see some success in this regard. Connecting with your soul tribe is on the cards this month as you create new connections and renew old ones.

Health

Health will be average but you will need to continue your efforts towards improving your health, stamina and energy levels. You need to focus on your health as a priority and realise that without health you won't be able to enjoy any other aspect of your life. You know what's right for you, it is time to listen to that inner guidance and follow it. Do not procrastinate and avoid these actions.

Spirituality

Anytime you find yourself not doing what you want to, notice the resistance and the inner voice that comes up. Notice the excuses the mind makes, pay attention to the words and sentences and know that it is the voice of your ego which is scared to be flexible or afraid of being wrong. Do not fight it, rather work along with it. It is just trying to protect you. Acknowledge the resistance and move past it.

September

Work

Work will be good and satisfying. Because of your efforts, plenty of good things are on the horizon but they are not here yet, so continue with your efforts. A partnership in business or work will prove to be very helpful and fruitful. If you have been planning to start a business with someone, this is a good time to take things ahead. Work will move ahead swiftly. Communication will be quick and easy.

Finances

Financially this is a good time. You are likely to be on top of things and in a position to make sound decisions. Don't get too stubborn about your ideas and be open to options as well. Your efforts at reaching out to people for investments will bear fruits this month. People see you as capable and trustworthy regarding their money. This is a good month to make some big financial decisions.

Love

In matters of love, you are likely to be worried about things people can do. But this worry is pointless because you have no control over others, only over your thoughts. Also the situation is not as bad as you think it is. You are likely to enjoy your solitude and alone time. If you have been looking for love, make sure you are actually open to having someone in your life. Otherwise it just leads to messy situations. Take your time.

Relationships

You are likely to reconnect with childhood friends and extended family members with whom you have had fond memories. This will be an enjoyable time and will be satisfying. Any inheritance matters are likely to be settled fairly, so you don't need to worry about it. Any disputes in the family will also be taken care of. Your urge to find connection with people who are not capable of giving that can lead to some disappointment.

Health

Health will be average. You have been exerting yourself a bit too much for some time now which can lead to exhaustion and burnout. It is time to take it easy on yourself and give your mind a break. Work with a therapist or a coach to help you deal with any blocks or past issues. Do not try to take any shortcuts with regards to your health. They will not help you in the long run.

Spirituality

Things that you have been working for are going to manifest in their own time. Just because something is taking time does not mean it is not going to happen. Avoid sharing your ideas, dreams or plans with anyone except for your cheerleaders. Plenty of activity is happening in the background. Take some time to quiet your mind and connect with universal intelligence. Really listen to it.

October

Work

Some big changes and important happenings are on the cards related to your work and career this month. The change is likely to be good and something you had been working for since quite some time. Even if you are in a leadership position, do not stop learning and growing. Share your ideas and learn from others as well. Your work is being appreciated and you will get your due rewards soon.

Finances

Financially this is likely to be a successful month as you are set to reap the rewards of your handwork very soon. Addition of income sources is likely to happen this month bringing surplus money at your disposal. Use it wisely. However, your efforts still need to continue as this is just the beginning. Any loans or partnerships that you had been working towards are likely to be successful and come to fruition.

Love

Some major changes are on the horizon for you in terms of very close relationships. If your relationship was toxic or not helping you grow, it can come to an end this month. Your work on healing your patterns of relationships is likely to bring a more evolved partner into your life. However, no matter how difficult the situation has been, do not take any rash decisions right now as they may backfire. Go with the flow and allow the things to take shape.

Relationships

Some relationships that have been unhealthy for you, you are likely to move away from them this month. You cannot compromise all your life and it's toxic for your health both physically and mentally. Choose to move away from unnecessary conflicts. But if confrontation is required, make sure to stand your ground as well. New and better people are likely to enter your life this month. Take this opportunity to get to know them.

Health

Health will be good. As you follow your doctor or expert's advice seriously, you will also begin to see the changes within you soon. What really helps your health is your decision to make it better. There may be periods when you get confused about what's working and what's not. Instead of letting that confusion influence your actions, speak to your expert and discuss with them. Don't be hesitant to see a counsellor or a coach to help you with the brain fog.

Spirituality

This is a time of taking some moments away from the busy schedule and doing nothing. When you are always doing something, you forgo the opportunity to really listen to your inner voice or the universe that is constantly speaking to you. In that listening you receive many answers to your questions as well as guidance. Spend some quiet moments listening to the guidance and then take action based on it boldly.

November

Work

This month work is likely to be slow. You could experience some delays and hurdles which can lead to feeling frustrated. It is important not to lose focus but keep doing your work. This is a good time to branch out into other fields if that has been your plan. For businesses, this month will be about reaching out to people and taking on different tasks. There could be some risk involved. So make sure you plan before you act.

Finances

Financially this month you may have to see some losses which can result in throwing your future plans into delays. The setbacks are more about forcing you to do some course correction especially if you had planned excessively beyond your capabilities. Don't let this disappointment stop your work. This is merely telling you your limits in the present. You will move away from this situation very soon if you keep your head on your shoulder firmly and don't let emotions get the better of you.

Love

In matters of love, this month you may not see much success especially if you are on the lookout for a suitable partner for marriage or even for dating. It is okay to be choosy and not compromise. Use your head and not just your heart when choosing the right partner for yourself. If you are in a steady relationship, you may have to find time from your busy schedule for your partner. If there are few things that you are not okay with, have an open communication instead of resenting quietly.

Relationships

Relationships will be more or less smooth and peaceful. You may have a difference of opinion with a friend or a close family member but don't let it affect your relationship. Do seek out help and guidance in this matter from someone who can have an impartial view. A marriage in the family is on the cards. It is likely to bring you closer to people with whom you haven't been in touch with. It is better to have a moderate approach to people instead of either being too pally or being too aloof.

Health

Health will be good this month. You will be able to make efforts towards improving your health and they will bring you good results as well. Any health issue that has been feeling like a big deal, you will be able to deal with with ease and also end up understanding more about your mental strength. Emotionally you may feel a bit low this month. Don't let this affect your relationships. Speak to a counsellor and help yourself through this emotional time.

Spirituality

You may end up feeling confused and unsure about your feelings and may also feel a lack of interest and purpose this month. This is the time to get your focus back. Pay attention to any nutritional deficiencies and focus on what is important for you. Use more affirmations and mirror work to help you move through this phase.

December

Work

This month is likely to be about new beginnings and opportunities. If you have been uninterested in your present organisation and have been looking for a new job, this month you will find success in this regard. A promotion is also on the cards. Plenty of changes are happening this month so it is important for you to know where your priorities lie. Think long term but focus on the present action that you need to take.

Finances

Financially this is likely to be a good month. Though the money inflow will be good, the expenses will also come knocking. You will have to play the balancing act and choose to spend wisely. You may feel burdened with responsibilities this month but you will be able to meet them with some effort. This is time to take proactive action towards your financial goals but avoid any rash decisions.

Love

In matters of love, this looks like a successful month. You will be able to find many suitable partners. But caution is also advised. Don't wear your heart on your sleeve. Be very thorough with what you really want in your relationship and what the other person brings to the table. Also be realistic about your expectations and also focus on what you bring to your relationship. If you have been feeling disappointed, it is time to have an open communication either with your partner or with yourself.

Relationships

Family and relationships will be a source of joy and comfort this month. You will receive much love and support as well as be in a position to give it equally back. There is a possibility of you getting stuck between two people who you love equally and could be asked to choose. Your diplomacy and truth will help you deal with it with ease. Often it is not about choosing but about being authentic about your expression of love.

Health

Health will be good. Any recovery from illness will be swift. Your efforts will be well rewarded. If you have been planning to start a health regimen, you may face difficulties in that. You could find yourself becoming inconsistent or losing motivation. It is better to have a partner in your journey, either a nutritionist or a personal trainer or even a coach to help you through.

Spirituality

It is the perfect time for you to start new projects, access new ideas and give birth to new conditions. You are in a fertile phase of life which means this is the right time for you to focus on manifesting your dreams and goals. If you have always wanted to turn your passion into a profession and spread your wisdom to others, do it now.

CHAPTER TWELVE

Aquarius

January 20–February 18

Overview

2023 is about learning to be optimistic and looking at the bright side of life. This year will test your faith in yourself and the universe. It will also teach you to go with the flow of life instead of trying to make things happen your way.

This year you are likely to find yourself in conflicts that can be easily avoided by a little foresight and understanding of others. Your ego may raise its head causing much trouble for you in your personal life. But if you consider it as a learning experience and understand that your ego is just a defence mechanism for you, you will be easily able to avoid many challenges and arguments.

In the professional arena, your drive and enthusiasm will help you move ahead with leaps and bounds. Professionally this year will be very successful for you and will establish your authority in your field of work. If you have plans for expansion of your business, especially overseas, this is the time to put them into action.

Studies abroad will be possible and bring good opportunities for you. Your preparation will decide the course and university but luck favours you in this regard. If you have been planning to settle overseas, then you may have to face some disappointment and delays in this matter.

Personally this year will bring up issues and challenges which will force you to look into your own patterns and expectations from people. You may want to get in touch with your feminine side of nurturing and caring qualities to mend and heal your deeper connections. Your loved ones may feel let down by your excessive focus on work, but it doesn't take much to please them. Stay away from buying peace with money and gifts. It is your time that will do that magic.

First half of the year is likely to be slow paced and potentially frustrating for you. But this is the time when you plan for the future and become ready for the new opportunities and the challenges it brings with itself. The second half of the year will see you getting into action and cutting through any obstacles and confusions. The universe is supporting you in many ways, all you have to do is to recognise it.

January

Work

You have plenty of new and refreshing ideas at work which will need some courage and planning to be implemented. If implemented they will be beneficial for you and those who work with you. You will be able to establish yourself as an authority in your field. A promotion or a change of position is on the cards. It is recommended to have a moderate approach to things. Do not try to go to extremes of either changing everything or doing nothing.

Finances

Finances will be good this month. You are likely to achieve success in a venture leading to increased income and better financial situation. Do not rush into any decisions related to money whether you are borrowing or lending. Think before you act or you could land in a soup. It is important to put things in black and white and pay attention to the fine print in major financial dealings.

Love

This is going to be a month of some major changes in your love life. This month marks a period of endings and new beginnings in your love life. It is time to let go of toxic or unhealthy relationships if they have been unfulfilling and brought more misery than joy. Relationship is supposed to be work but it is definitely not all work and no joy. If you are seeking out a partner, you will come across someone who captures your attention and makes you feel joy.

Relationships

In the area of relationships in general too, this month is likely to bring in plenty of changes. On the face of it, it may seem like a difficult time. But it also ushers in the new energy bringing with it people who really do respect your boundaries and make an effort to understand you. Don't be afraid to reach out to those who you can connect with ease.

Health

Health will be good and will support you in your endeavours. This month marks the closure in many ways, one of them being complete or almost complete recovery from an illness or an injury. Your restraint has helped you achieve your health goals and will go a long way in helping you maintain a certain routine and discipline in your life. It is important to receive ideas and help in this regard.

Spirituality

Abundance is a state of mind. It is not just about money, but also about supportive people around you and a healthy lifestyle. This month the universe urges you to focus on thoughts of abundance, especially about what you want rather than what you don't want. Sometimes, receiving is a bigger challenge than giving. It is time you learn to receive with grace and gratitude.

February

Work

In terms of work you will need to work as a part of the team to get the results instead of being a one man army. Though you believe you work best alone, yet there are benefits to working as a team. They can be your cheerleaders, supporters as well as critics helping you fine-tune your work and bringing out the best in you often. Do not escape from difficult situations, they will follow you no matter what. It is better to face it once and for all.

Finances

Financially this month will be a mixed bag. You are in the right mindset of taking wise and well-thought decisions regarding money and investments. But you may have to bear some losses too from a bad investment in the past. Good news is that it won't affect your financial situation to a great extent. Allow your partner or people in your life to support and help you either financially or in making sound financial decisions whether of lending or investing.

Love

In matters of love, you will need to be more mind oriented than heart centred this month. You have to see the truth of the person, not just their potential. This requires clear insight and a sense of what's important for you now. You may find it difficult this month to manage your personal and professional life and strike a balance. Don't let this make you overcompensate in your love life as it could lead to problems later on. Clear communication is the need of the hour.

Relationships

Some relationships can be confusing for you as their words and actions don't match and your expectations are quite different from them. Instead of getting into this confusion, give it some time until you reach a point of having more information and clarity. It is important not to over-commit yourself to any engagements this month as you may find yourself in a tight spot later on. Stay playful, enjoy your time with friends and don't plan too much in advance.

Health

Health will be average this month. You are likely to stick to your health and exercise program and routine which will give you good results. But you will need to wait. This is the time to just do your best. Any recovery from illness is going to be slow but sure. Have patience. Do not overthink and certainly don't let any fears cloud your judgments. Practice mindfulness for better sleep.

Spirituality

In order to find motivation and purpose, focus on what drives you, what makes you wake up every morning in a pleasant way and propels you to work effortlessly. This will mean letting go of past ideas and conditionings and focussing on the present, the truth of who you really are and what you actually enjoy doing. If your answer to this is "I don't know", then it's time for you to start exploring it.

March

Work

Work this month will be smooth flowing. You are likely to receive accolades for your efforts in the past. A job offer or a meeting that you have been waiting for is likely to happen this month. Your insight and guidance can be helpful for your colleagues and employees. Be generous with it and give it graciously. Stay away from indulging in any ego games or contests as there is not going to be any winner but losers. Find an amicable way of resolving conflicts.

Finances

Finances this month will be good. You may experience a stagnation or slow down in the pace of money flow. It is time to nurture what you have instead of spending mindlessly. Be cautious of capacity expansion unless planned very thoroughly. New ideas can be implemented after planning and examination.

Love

In terms of love, this month will be good. Your search for a partner is likely to be successful. If you have been meaning to ask someone out, take the step as luck is on your side. It is time to bring more love and passion into your relationship. Don't wait for your partner to do something special always. You can also be the one to do it this time.

Relationships

The theme of endings and new beginnings continues in your relationships this month as well. You may see some people moving away. You may have to spend some time alone before those who are aligned and resonate with you can enter your life. This is time for some major cleansing inside and outside in your personal life. Don't be afraid to reach out to a coach or a therapist for help if things get overwhelming.

Health

Health will be okay. You will need to make some extra efforts into maintaining good health this month. Work on improving your immunity levels and keeping allergens at bay. Working with a doctor or a nutritionist or a trainer can be very helpful this month and will enable you to better your physical body. If you have been suffering from an illness, the right diagnosis is important to heal. Reach out for a second opinion if necessary.

Spirituality

This month brings you lessons in detachment and letting go. It is imperative to understand and learn the difference between numbing out, indifference and detachment. Any spiritual path that resonates with you will help you deal with what's going on in your emotional life. Take some time out to go to a meditation or a spiritual retreat for some time this month.

April

Work

You may find yourself faced with unexpected hurdles and delays at the workplace. Some projects may get delayed and you may have to readjust the timelines, so be mentally prepared for that. Conflicts at the workplace due to petty ego issues can escalate into something big, so stay clear of this as much as possible. If you have been looking for a job, you are likely to receive something good but you may have to compromise on an important aspect. Choose wisely.

Finances

Financially this will be a good month as you are poised to receive a promotion or a hike which will make your situation and position as per your expectation. You will also be in a position to help others through some financial difficulties, don't hesitate to help. Any investments or borrowings for business need to be looked at carefully before proceeding with it. You are in the right frame of mind to make good financial decisions.

Love

In terms of love, this month could put a damper on your plans as things or relationships may not turn out to be what you had expected. If you are meeting new people for dating or potential partners, keep an open mind and don't put many expectations on the first meeting or first person you meet. Plenty of dynamics are changing for you personally, be open to forgiving and letting go of the past.

Relationships

If you wonder why people don't respond well to your genuine well-meaning gestures, perhaps you also need to look at the people for whom you are doing those actions. Sometimes, they are not in a state or don't have the capacity to be what you want from them. You do not have to consider everyone as your friend. Some people can stay on as acquaintances or just a family member. Understand and learn the difference.

Health

Health will need care this month. If you have been ignoring warning signs regarding your health, it is time you began to pay attention to them. It is possible that you are perceiving something as very big or difficult but in reality, on examination it turns out to be something benign or easily curable. Instead of jumping to conclusions, let the doctor do their job.

Spirituality

If you keep ignoring what your heart wants, you will eventually not be able to listen to yourself at all. This month, spend some time really listening and introspecting. New ways and journeys are opening up for you. It is time to look at the path which you have wanted to follow but never knew or never had the courage.

May

Work

Work is likely to flow smoothly and things will speed up as you rush to meet your deadlines. Keep your communication lines open for potential clients or employees and peers who may need your support and guidance. Don't get fazed with any disappointments because you cannot control everything. Stay flexible in your approach. A celebration is on the cards related to the workplace.

Finances

Financially this month will be average. You may have to face some delays in payments and money inflows for which you will need to borrow some funds. The process will happen smoothly but your flexibility and adaptability in approach will go a long way in making sure things happen easily. You will be able to meet your financial commitments.

Love

Beggars can't be choosers and as long as you beg for love and affection, you are likely to stay in the cycle of misery and anger. If you are looking for love, you will have to find time for it from your busy schedule. Let go of fear and doubts because you will manifest what you focus on. In your steady relationships, it is time to take them to the next level. Don't be afraid of taking any major steps in this direction.

Relationships

Relationships are likely to be good this month. As some people move out of your life, you may find yourself indulging in nostalgia and remembering the old days with fondness. But when an empty space is created, new and better people come in. Welcome them with open arms and moderate expectations. It is also time for you to begin to set healthy boundaries with friends and family.

Health

Health will need more attention this month. Be careful when doing any strenuous physical activity or driving. You may have to give yourself some time to recover from an illness or an injury. Basically life is asking you to slow down and be present in this moment. Seek out a health professional - either a nutritionist or a coach, to help you in your emotional healing journey.

Spirituality

If you spend too much worrying about the future or thinking about the past, then that is what you are going to attract more of in your life. What is in the past is over, you cannot change it. Regretting it is not going to help. It is time for you to learn to forgive and move on. Closure doesn't have to happen from someone else. It can also happen when you decide you are done with it.

June

Work

Work will be slow this month as it will need more planning before execution. It is better to get it right once than to do it again. If you have been waiting for an opportunity at work, it can take some time but good things are on the horizon. You will need to stay focussed and have laser-like clarity in order to do your job perfectly. Do not shirk your responsibility or compromise on the quality of work as it will show badly for you.

Finances

Financially this is likely to be a good month. Money inflows will be abundant and expenses will be in proportion but you will be able to monitor and control it as much as possible. This is the time to save and invest in secure places rather than take risks as you may have to utilise it later on. If you can delay certain expenses, you should do that this month.

Love

Even though you are open to receiving a new loving partner into your life, yet you also seem to be carrying the wounds from the past. This will affect the quality of your relationship. It is time to heal it and let it go. Not every experience and not every person is going to hurt you. If your expectations are not being met, perhaps it is also prudent to see if your expectations are realistic enough for others.

Relationships

Relationships are a two-way street. It involves give and take of love, feelings, communication and everything else. It is time to create that balance. If you are being stubborn or too critical of yourself or others, it can create problems in your relationships. Things and people don't have to be the way you want, stay flexible and embrace the diversity and differences as they can teach you many different perspectives of life.

Health

Health will be average. It is getting better and will improve with time and effort. You just need to have some patience with yourself and trust the healing process. It is time to let go of any limitations that you may have placed on yourself physically or mentally. Reach out and do something actively for your physical health. Fresh air will be rejuvenating and healing.

Spirituality

This is the time when ego raises its head and can cause some problems for you without you realising. You only need to shed some light on it, look at yourself objectively and do some introspection to clear it up. Be willing to do that and don't let it interfere in your relations.

July

Work

Work this month will be satisfying and you will be able to succeed in fulfilling expectations from you at the workplace. You are likely to receive your dues and if you have been looking forward to a raise or promotion, it is very likely to happen this month. This is a good time to look at expanding your business or your client base as you are ready for new opportunities.

Finances

Financially this month will be stable with steady income and gains. Expenses are likely to be on the higher side, yet you will be able to save and control your expenditure. There is a possibility of a decision that needs to be made and it is going to be difficult to choose between two similar choices. It will be best to consult experts about it instead of trying to do this on your own. It is better to make the decision as soon as possible.

Love

You will need to have clarity about what you want in your relationship from your partner, whether you are looking for a partner or you are in a steady relationship. If you are confused between two individuals, it is better to wait until the decision becomes clear or just take a decision and make it right. The longer you stay in this indecisiveness, the more complicated it will become.

Relationships

Relationships will be overall peaceful and be a source of comfort and joy for you. It is time to let go of your assumptions about certain people and really look at the truth about them. Family gatherings and get-togethers are on the cards. Matters of inheritance may also come up which are likely to be decided in the near future. Immediate family may not support you in certain decisions related to marriage. Weigh the pros and cons before going ahead with any decision.

Health

Health is likely to be a bit problematic this month. If you have been postponing your regular health checkups, it is time to get it done and pay attention and address any issues that might get highlighted. It is best to have a moderate approach to life and habits, any excesses will cause more problems related to digestion like acidity, bloating and increased heat in the body. Keep stress levels in control by practising breathwork and meditation.

Spirituality

It is important to remember for you that any love that is conditional and based on a transaction is not essentially love. This is the right time for you to explore unconditional love. The best way to do it is to begin by recognising it outside of you in the world. Begin to express it for others without expecting anything in return. You will realise the beauty of it and the calmness it brings with it.

August

Work

This month you need to put your personal insecurities aside and learn to work in collaboration with your team as that is what will bring you good results. Remember it is not competition but cooperation that brings best results for all. Stay away from any ego battles and be open to learning new things everyday. This is the time for you to stay away from saying any harsh words in the heat of the moment that you could regret later on.

Finances

Financial situation will be good, yet there is likely to be some stress around money and cash inflows which could escalate tensions within you. It is possible that the situation is not as bad as you are thinking or making it to be. Stay calm and allow the solutions to emerge. This is not the right time to make investments or increase them especially in speculative and risky instruments.

Love

In matters of love, you are going to see some success this month. You have the mental clarity regarding what you want, what you can give and what you expect from your partner. It will be even better if you can learn to communicate it to them with clarity as well. Things will materialise but there is a waiting period. Allow your connection to be nurtured before it can grow. Be willing to take proactive steps in your relationship.

Relationships

This month you may be torn between spending time with your loved ones and taking some alone time out for yourself. You may need to pick one over another as your efforts towards balancing or doing both may not be fruitful and can lead to more problems than solutions. A happy addition to the family is on the cards. You may decide to go on a vacation either alone or with a loved one.

Health

You have been worrying too much and it is beginning to show up in your other areas of life including your health. You may experience insomnia, increased stress levels, anxiety and low immunity. Take a break from the hustle bustle of life and spend some time in nature to heal your sensibilities and unwind. Spending time with someone who makes you feel loved and comfortable including pets will be very healing for you.

Spirituality

Take some quiet time alone to rest, meditate and contemplate this month. When confused, it is imperative to take a few moments and deep breaths to clear your mind. Learning and practising breath work, day dreaming or doing something creative that brings on the meditative state for you will be rejuvenating for you.

September

Work

This month you need to be careful about your immediate circle and who you share your plans with about your business and future projects as there may be someone around you who is not happy about your progress and can have a destructive mindset. It is also time to evaluate your worth and whether it's time to break through the glass ceiling in your present line of work/job or seek something else.

Finances

Financially this month can present some challenges regarding increased expenses compared to the income. You may tend to indulge in impulsive spending and buy things which you don't really need. Keep a check on this habit or you could easily over-extend your budget and then face problems with credit. If you are not doing it already, start setting aside a small amount every month for either savings or urgent expenses.

Love

Though you may want to do the right thing by your partner, yet if you have been feeling a certain disconnect with them emotionally, perhaps it's time to re-evaluate your relationship and what you need from them. Don't let disappointments affect you so much that you feel hopeless because there is still a lot to look forward to. It's just about shifting your perspective to seeing what's working or the blessing in the situation.

Relationships

Relationships could be challenging this month as you struggle to identify who is being your friend and who is just pretending to be. You have the insight to make better decisions, just don't second guess yourself or doubt your judgement about it. You may want to connect with an old friend or someone from extended family just as you connect with them in the past, but you need to acknowledge that time has moved on and things can be different now.

Health

Health will be good this month. You will generally feel optimistic and have the energy - both physically and mentally - to deal with anything that life throws at you. If you have been dealing with a chronic illness, this is a sign that the treatment is working and will soon bring positive results. Stay on the course and keep doing the positive things for your health.

Spirituality

You may experience complacency in certain areas of life. While it is good for sometime, you will need to shake it off and move ahead with renewed vigour. If you find yourself lacking in inspiration or purpose, then focus on finding that. Ideally, your purpose is something you are passionate about in life. Be honest with yourself. What is the heart's true desire? Focus on that.

October

Work

Opportunities at work and new business opportunities are opening up this month. Instead of worrying about things, it is time to take action and work towards materialising them. Don't be afraid to ask for help and learn new things to upgrade yourself. A new career path may be opening for you and if that is what you have been waiting for, then this is the right time to explore it.

Finances

Financially, this will be a good month overall. There may be some payments or lending which may not come back in the way you expected. It may feel like a loss but new sources of income are likely to open up for you. This is not the time to look back at what you lost but to look ahead at what you stand to gain. Keep up your efforts and do not be discouraged by the temporary setbacks.

Love

If you are looking for love, this is not likely to be a fruitful month. You may end up meeting many prospects but none that you can resonate with. It is better to wait than settle for someone who is not the right match for you. If you are in a steady relationship, you may experience some challenges which you will need to work on to resolve them. Don't be afraid of being vulnerable and sharing your true feelings.

Relationships

Relationships will be overall positive. You need to stop paying attention to the problems and start focussing on the good that is there. If you want to heal your relationship with someone, you need to focus on why that relationship is important for you and what you like about that person. You do not have to sacrifice your values in order to relate to someone.

Health

Health will be average. This is the time to pay attention to any health issues that may come up. Focus on improving your immunity levels as it will help you in keeping up your general health. Stay away from any addictions and addictive substances as it will only create more problems for you in terms of health as well as other areas of life. Focus on healing yourself emotionally and harmonising your heart and mind.

Spirituality

You may be fascinated by the so-called "spiritual" things like clairvoyance and telepathy. But focussing on them will lead you away from true spiritual growth and evolution. It is time for you to meet the right people and move out of your comfort zone. Real spirituality is about having a different perspective of life.

November

Work

This month you will need to work hard and sometimes even extend hours to meet your deadlines and reach your goals. However, your results may not be as per your efforts. Don't let this discourage you as your hard work will be rewarded and appreciated in ways that you didn't imagine soon. Be confident about yourself and your capabilities and learn to present it to others without hesitation. It is not boasting but a true representation of your efforts.

Finances

Financially this month is likely to be good. An inheritance matter may take up your time and effort but it will bring fruitful results eventually. Do not allow yourself to be complacent and don't focus on what's not working as it will jeopardise your efforts. Mental clarity and precise planning will be helpful this month as you work towards creating more abundance and ease in your life.

Love

In terms of love, this month will be fruitful and you are likely to find your soulmate and a good match. But there may be delays in decision making creating more stress and anxiety for you. On one hand you will want to move ahead with speed and get done with things but on the other hand you will be riddled with doubts and fears. It is time to make the decision and know that every person has good and bad things. It is only about what you can work with.

Relationships

You will find yourself having an upper hand in your relationships this month. There may be a power struggle with people around you but you will know how to deal with it in a manner that's amicable and peaceful. You are in a good position to guide others in the family about certain things and people look forward to seeking advice from you. If you are struggling with issues related to fertility and childbirth, this is an auspicious month and you are likely to see good results.

Health

Health will be good this month. You will still need to keep making consistent efforts and steadily keep working towards your health and fitness goals. Being flexible about your time but not compromising on your fitness regimen will be good for you. Family will support you in your healing journey but you will be the one taking steps. Don't expect them to understand your struggles rather you are the one who has to stand for what you know is right and do it.

Spirituality

You seem to be struggling with life and yourself when in fact there is no real need for that. Acknowledge the ease with which things have happened for you and look forward to that. The universe is pouring its abundance out to you. Be open to receiving.

December

Work

This month some projects are coming to a close and many things will fall in place for you to move ahead with ease and a sense of completion. However, there may be phases when you may feel a sense of loss about things that didn't happen or opportunities that didn't convert. It is time to give birth to the ideas that you have been gestating for some time now. This month, just like the year end, is also about endings and new beginnings in your workplace.

Finances

Finances will be average. Your hard work is paying off in terms of finances and money inflow which you will begin to see the results soon.

Some expenses on family or upgrading your home may come up which, although a bit out of your budget, will bring much satisfaction to you. Instead of worrying about it, it is better to enjoy it and then focus on abundance instead of the expenses.

Love

In terms of love, this month may not be as good especially if you are looking for love. You may end up encountering people who can bring up some toxic patterns in your life. Be careful of any red flags and don't wait for it to turn into a carnival of red flags before taking an action. If you are in a steady relationship, things will be much more peaceful and steady.

Relationships

You may want to have a certain kind of relationship with friends and family but you need to acknowledge that time and circumstances have changed which inevitably lead to change in the dynamics and personalities. Do not try to get too close nor reject people outright. Stay moderate in your approach and don't expect everyone to behave in the same way they did in the past.

Health

Health will be average and will need constant care and attention. If you are not happy with a diagnosis you have received, seek a second opinion and be optimistic about the treatment plan. Things don't always have to work your way to be effective. Be flexible and allow others to do their job. Your results will be in line with your efforts towards your health.

Spirituality

If you feel like you have been at the wrong side of the bargain in life and situations, then it is time to rethink. You have many things that work for you. Count your blessings. Help is always available if only you are willing to ask for it. You are stronger than you think you are. If you want a happy outcome, focus on abundance, not the lack of it.

CHAPTER THIRTEEN

Pisces

February 19–March 20

Overview

2023 is about change in every area of life for Pisceans. Change is usually associated with something bad. But it is in fact a very important part of life because without change one becomes stagnant and irrelevant. This year you are likely to see changes in the way you look at life and how life responds to you.

This year you will be prompted to express your ideas and put them into action. But it will also mean you will have to be open to criticism from those around you. In face of it, you will need to trust yourself, your ideas and keep moving ahead with confidence and a sense of knowing what you are trying to do.

This year you are likely to be involved in collaborations and team projects. This is an area which comes easily to those born under the Pisces sign. However, it will also mean you need to take accountability for your role and not be complacent about your work. Some people are likely to move out of your life who do not agree with your ideology and new people will find their way in your life.

Personally this year will be overall peaceful as you enjoy the support and company of people who you consider close to you. Socially you will be active and will enjoy the time spent with friends and family. You will also be a mentor and guide for those around you who are beginning their journey in life.

Professionally this year will be about networking and connecting with people. You cannot just work and expect people to know about it and appreciate it. You will need to put yourself out there and become visible. If it is a challenge for you, then face it head on. Own your brilliance.

First half of the year will be more about learning new skills and adjusting to a new way of life and being. It is going to require your efforts and energy as well as resourcefulness. Relocation is also possible. Second half of the year will be about reaping the rewards of your hard work. You will find yourself in a place of achievement and establish your presence. Childbirth and marriage are also on the cards for some of you.

January

Work

This month will be excellent regarding work. New opportunities are on the horizon. Promotions, recognition are on the cards. You will have an optimistic outlook towards life and career which will help you make the best use of your available opportunities. Business expansion plans are best finalised now so that they can be implemented soon. If you have been looking for an ideal career path, you will find something that interests you and is aligned to your purpose.

Finances

Financially this month can be somewhat challenging as you deal with some losses and there is a sense that you have to begin from scratch in some places. Though it may feel like a very bleak outlook, yet there are many good things happening, focus on them. Staying optimistic will help you ride through difficult times. Stay away from lending money and trusting people blindly as it could backfire.

Love

In matters of love, this month will be good. You are likely to experience and seek out more stability in your relationship and that is going to be a driving force for you. Even though you like to flow with things, yet the need for certainty and stability drives many of your relationship decisions in life. It is best not to be too stubborn and rigid. Try to have a flexible perspective when relating to someone in your life.

Relationships

You will need skill and logic to navigate the landscape of relationships as they can prove somewhat challenging this month. You may be dealing with making decisions about certain people in your life and how you relate to them. You tend to think in extremes, but it is best to have a moderate approach and not to treat everything like ripping off a bandaid. You can look through other's intentions, use this insight to understand how to relate to people.

Health

Health will be good. Yet you may experience burnout or exhaustion at times during this month. Honour your energy levels and instead of being too harsh on yourself, give your body the kind of rest it needs for rejuvenation. Energy work, energy healing and alternative medicine and healing therapies will prove to be very beneficial.

Spirituality

It is time to connect with your inner nurturing aspect and give that to yourself. You tend to help others without giving yourself what you need the most. Remember, you can't help someone with an empty cup. Fill yours first. There is no need to worry and everything will work out beautifully. You don't have to fixate on fixing someone else.

February

Work

Work will be a balancing act this month as you struggle to deal with professional and personal issues along with expanding business propositions all at the same time. You may feel overwhelmed, don't hesitate to reach out for support. This is not the time to complete tasks and compromise on their quality as it will be harmful for your reputation. Perhaps learning to say NO will ease plenty of your burdens this month.

Finances

Financially this month may be a bit difficult. Though the income is steady, mounting expenses and impulse buying can really throw you off balance. This is a good time to understand the difference between your needs and wants and prioritise better. You may experience some losses in certain investments. Guidance is to not focus on what you lost, but on what you have and what you gained from that experience.

Love

In matters of love, this month will be quiet and slow. You have plenty of ideas on how to woo the person of your interest or your spouse, but implementing those ideas may prove to be a challenge. This month, no matter how fast you try to move and act, things may not go as per your expectations and pace. Allow yourself to calm down and move at a pace which is more comfortable.

Relationships

Your relationships seem to be undergoing an overhaul. Plenty of people who pull you down will soon leave your life and many who uplift you will come back. This however is not an easy process. It is accompanied by its own set of challenges and heartbreak. You may feel let down, unable to share your deepest thoughts with anyone and feel a sense of uncertainty regarding people in your life. Allow this change to happen as it will bring in souls that are aligned to you.

Health

Health seems to be getting better but still you are fighting with demons that are more in the mind and are subconscious. Life is offering you a chance to work on your health. This is a good time to learn to strike a balance between your personal and professional life. If you are struggling with a health issue, the cause is most likely emotional. Focus on healing the emotional aspect of it to find balance and harmony.

Spirituality

You are blossoming into a new being. As this has been your prayer for such a long time, allow this blossoming to happen. Learn to give as much as you like to receive. Open the channels of flow so that blessings and guidance can flow through your life with ease. Have patience with yourself and the process and do not give up.

March

Work

Work will move at a fast pace this month. Stuck projects and ventures will come to life and progress is on the cards. A communication that you have been waiting for some time is likely to come bearing good news this month. Trips and travel related to work are likely to occupy a majority of your time. While it will be fruitful, it will also provide you a new direction for your work and growth.

Finances

Financially this month will be average. Income stays steady but expenses will mount leading to an imbalance and stress. Certain unexpected outflows of money can throw your budget off balance. This is a good time to add multiple sources of income for yourself and you will find success in this regard. If your money is being spent on a source or an avenue that has not yielded any fruitful results, then it's time to reconsider it.

Love

In terms of love, this will be a successful and beautiful month. You are likely to meet new people and if you are in search of your soulmate, there is a high probability you will find yours this month. An ex might show up in your life. Though the memories and association may have been fond, remember the reasons why it is ex and do not get swayed by it. For those in a steady relationship, it is time to take your relationship to the next level.

Relationships

Relationships overall will be difficult to handle. But you are learning to move away from the drama and the toxic elements. It is time to leave your past and your troubles behind as a lot of good things are waiting for you. This is the time to attract the kind of people you have always wanted in your life. Your social life could get hectic which means a juggling act or a balancing act will be required.

Health

Health will be average but a good thing that's happening is you will begin to look after yourself more carefully. You will find the time and motivation to heal yourself, have a healthy lifestyle and stick to it. A good hearty workout will be possible and helpful. There is a need for discipline in your life and you will be able to cultivate it this month.

Spirituality

You have been busy in the worldly life for some time now and have completely neglected your spiritual aspect. But this also leads to a disconnect with your purpose and passion. Find time everyday to connect with yourself, for meditation and inner dialogue. Be honest with yourself and focus on your purpose if you ever feel demotivated or lost.

April

Work

Work will be smooth and satisfying this month. You may find yourself becoming somewhat complacent with your position and work. This could lead to troubles in the future. Shake the complacency, shift your gears and move to the next level. Challenge yourself and work towards fulfilling it. You do not have to make things very easy or extremely difficult. It has to be just right, just one step out of your comfort zone.

Finances

Finances will be good this month as you take charge of it with diligence and a firm hand. Unnecessary expenses may come up this month but your patience and foresight will be able to take care of it with ease. If you are looking to turn around your venture that has been going into losses or you have not been financially viable, this is the right time to look into it.

Love

In the matter of seeking love, you may have to face some disappointment this month. You tend to get attached to the wrong person sometimes, not realising that they are not into the relationship as much as you are. It is better to learn to let go of those who are not invested and make room for those who can be. For those in a steady relationship, you can take things for granted sometimes. You need to be more proactive in your acts of love towards your partner.

Relationships

Relationships will be stable as you learn to take control of your life and choose who stays and who leaves. You are in a place where people will expect your help and guidance. While you do that open heartedly, also remember to see that one who genuinely needs your help receives it and stay away from those who don't want to take responsibility for themselves. Your ideas and suggestions can help many around you lead a better life and receive guidance.

Health

Health will be good as you take charge of yourself and your lifestyle. Following and sticking to a health program of food and workout will help you with increased energy levels, immunity, and strength. If you have been struggling to recover from an illness or an infection, you will find health and healing this month.

Spirituality

Though you have moved on in life in many aspects and ways, yet you may sometimes feel stuck and bound in a mental attitude which can be difficult to shake off. But the good news is, it's just in the mind now. It's no more your reality. Let go of anything that stops you from growing and evolving and move ahead with confidence as the universe supports you in all your endeavours.

May

Work

This month will be about taking stock of things and situations at the workplace as this will decide your path ahead in your career. If you have been struggling with a job or a line of career and have been contemplating making the switch, this is the time to start planning for it. It will take some time to materialise and show up as a fruitful opportunity, so patience will be a virtue for you this month. Don't make any rash decisions.

Finances

Financially this is a month to start planning future investments and growth strategies. Money will flow in with as much speed as it flows out. It can get frustrating but do not rush into cutting off any expenses without giving it some thought and consideration. You may have to curb some unnecessary expenditures which will benefit your lifestyle and health as well. Move ahead with confidence without fear of finances as it will be taken care of.

Love

As new love enters your life, ask yourself if you are ready for it or are you still stuck in the past expecting the worst to happen. What happened once is not bound to repeat. Allow love to come into your life, let yourself embrace it but with open arms and open eyes. You have been planning to make some decision regarding your love life, this is the time to do it. The longer you wait, the more difficult it gets.

Relationships

Relationships seem to be a challenging area for you this year. While there are plenty of good things happening in your personal life, yet a part of you still fears the worst. People and events may show up in your life that correspond to how you were in the past, but trust yourself that you have changed and you can handle things much better and much more calmly now.

Health

Health will be average as you try to create more balance in your life and take some time out from your busy schedule. An old health problem may rear its head. Remember to heed to it as it arises as prevention is better than cure. Water therapies will be healing for the body and calming for the mind as water is also your base element, Pisces being a water sign. Stream, sauna, swimming, dip in the pool or an extended bath in the bathtub or something as simple as dipping your feet in a bucket of water with some salt.

Spirituality

If you worry about being dealt the wrong hand or being at the receiving end of injustice, remember that your life and how you react to it depends on you. Learn to honour yourself as that teaches others to honour you. Consider yourself as worthy of love, abundance and justice. Expect miracles and know that it can happen for you also.

June

Work

This month at the work front, you may feel as if some of your choices are backfiring. But in reality, it is just a lack of organisation, skill and inability to ask for and receive help. You have the capability, but it is time to build the requisite skill. Invest in yourself. Don't indulge in self-pity if your work is suffering. Work out ways to find your passion and drive for what you do. Things are not as bad as they may seem.

Finances

Financially the situation will be average, but you may feel that being dependent on one source can be uncertain and tricky. At the same time, what you need right now is focus. So avoid the temptation of stretching yourself too thin and prioritise your needs and goals. This may require you to take a break from the hustle bustle of the mind and retreat to reorganise your mind.

Love

In terms of love, this month will have mixed results. If you are in a steady relationship, this month will bring you much joy and comfort from your partner. But if you have been in a toxic relationship and have been considering letting it go, then consider this your sign to do it. If you are looking for love, this month may not be very fruitful and lucky. Have patience and don't let your hopes down.

Relationships

Relationships can be disappointing for you. But the good news is that you finally come to terms with who is your well-wisher and who isn't. So it becomes easier for you to let go of those who don't add value to your life in any way. You have to face some tough choices but this is a choice you can't really escape from. Avoid going into any extremes of behaviour and don't take things too personally.

Health

Health will be good and will support you in other areas of life. Your efforts will bear the fruits and it will bring you great satisfaction. If you are facing a health issue or are stuck in your wellness journey, consult an expert or a doctor and do not try to self-medicate or diagnose. This is the time you need external help as you won't have all the information needed to help you. The weather will assist you and help you heal faster.

Spirituality

Patience is an undervalued virtue. It is talked about a lot but not many really know it. This is your time to cultivate and have patience as it will help you grow from within. Even when you plant seeds, you need to have patience for it to grow, flower and evolve. Remember that when you are nurturing yourself. You know what to do. Trust your inner wisdom .

July

Work

Work this month will be slow. Many changes are happening at the workplace which can be somewhat challenging and seem difficult. It is not the time to think about what is not there but on what can be created now in this present day. If you have been looking for a change in job or career or a completely different field of business, this is the right time for it. It is time to upgrade yourself or learn a new skill. Stay optimistic.

Finances

Financially though things will be fine yet there is likely to be some uncertainty which can throw you off balance. Stay grounded. You are being looked after by the universe and you are also in a position to handle your life and finances with ease. It is time to prioritise yourself and your requirements. Stay away from lending someone money or investing it in ambitious schemes.

Love

Even though you want to be optimistic, yet you may feel an apathy towards love and relationships. It could be disillusionment. But this is not the reality of the situation. Good things are happening if only you are willing to look at it with an open heart. It is time for endings and new beginnings. Don't linger on what was for so long that you miss out on what is and what can be.

Relationships

You are being constantly reminded of making yourself a priority and trusting your instincts. It is only when you don't listen to your gut and ignore the red flags in relationships that it creates more problems in your life. Learn to set boundaries, reach out to people who will honour you and want you in their life instead of those who only want to benefit themselves at your cost. You don't have to be a doormat for genuine well-wishers to accept you.

Health

Health will be good. It is time to be optimistic instead of mulling over the why's of certain problems. Be solution oriented. There is no point in worrying over health problems to the point of having sleepless nights full of worries and anxiety. Reach out for help. Be willing to receive guidance. Alternative medicine and counselling will be very helpful.

Spirituality

You need to stop worrying about everything in your life. Worry is also a form of prayer. It is time to take your power back from others and take control of your life and choices. If you ever find yourself blaming someone else for your problems or circumstances, just shift the narrative to "What can I do about this?" This will completely change your energy and your situations.

August

Work

You will be able to find your feet in your work and career and be grounded enough to build upon it. If you have been planning to be an entrepreneur and starting a new venture, then this is the perfect time to move in this direction. It is better to go solo until you have clarity about how you want to work and your vision. There are likely to be some difficulties with employees and clients, but you will be easily able to handle it.

Finances

Financially this will be a tricky month as you will have to be on top of the expenses and be very practical about where money is being spent. You may want to explore investment options that are safe and flexible. But it is your time to gradually move away from any financial problems. Your astute planning and foresight will be helpful and take care of any unexpected expenditures.

Love

In matters of love, this is likely to be a disappointing month. If you are looking for forgiveness, you may end up meeting many people but none that would be up to your expectations. Perhaps it's time for you to look within and notice what it is that you exactly want from a relationship and the other person and what it is that you can bring to it. If you are in a steady relationship, some miscommunication can be expected. Having clarity and taking time out for it will help.

Relationships

Relationships this month will be average. People look up to you for support and guidance rather than the other way around. This can mean you will need to find time for yourself as well in the midst of all that is happening in life. You may go on a solo trip this month which will be very rejuvenating for your senses. It is time to pick and choose people in your life who uplift you and bring a positive impact on you.

Health

Health will be average. You may experience certain problems associated with low immunity. It is time to pay attention to your environment and get rid of any allergens if possible. Don't hesitate in taking a second opinion and seeking help from someone who can save your time and effort. You may feel low on energy. Meditation, a good nutritious diet and fresh air will be beneficial.

Spirituality

You may want to reminisce about the past but it is also prudent to remember that it is over and the only time you have is the present. It is time to leave the comfort zone and step into some uncertain waters of life to explore what's beyond the boundary of your mind. Unleash your adventurous side, take risks and be daring. Growth lies outside your comfort zone.

September

Work

Work can be a bit slow and unpredictable this month. You may have to juggle between more than one job or projects which can leave you feeling exhausted and overwhelmed. But it is not the work but the mental pressure and uncertainty about things that is making you feel like that. Allow yourself to receive help that is available to you. All you have to do is look for it and have patience.

Finances

Financially this month may seem a bit difficult. You may have to work more than usual to make ends meet. Money can get stuck in the most unlikely of places. So avoid lending money and investing more than you are comfortable. This is not the time for grand plans and expansion. It is time to plan and wait for the right time to take action. Diligence and consistency will help you ride through the situation.

Love

You may have to face a betrayal or disappointment in love this month. Perhaps you already had the inkling of it but you may have chosen to ignore the gut instincts and the red flags. Take some time to ponder over why it happened and your role in it. Look within to heal your grief instead of moving on to another relationship. For those in a steady relationship, this month will bring more stability into your life and you could even plan ahead.

Relationships

Relationships will be good as long you understand and stick to the boundaries. You are in a position to help people around you with guidance and support and they will ask for it too. But remember to help only those who genuinely require it and are willing to work and help themselves. This is not the time for charity. Be wise in your spending over your loved ones. Your guidance will be much more valuable than any other help.

Health

Health will be good. You may experience stress headaches and other stress related issues, but it is not something that you cannot help. Overall health will be good and any illness is on recovery. It is time to choose to prioritise your health and yourself over others. Your choice will determine the quality of your life in years to come.

Spirituality

While it may seem like a difficult time to be in, yet this is an ending and a beginning of sorts. It is the beginning of another new journey where you can learn from your mistakes and use them to build a better life. The universe is pouring its abundance and is willing to help you in every step. All you have to do is be willing to make the journey and take the help.

October

Work

Work will be good as new opportunities come your way and show you a new direction. This is the month to work hard and diligently towards your goal. Whether you are just starting out or thinking of expanding your business, this is the right time to look for collaborations and partnerships that can help you grow as a team. If you have wanted to turn your passion into a profession, this is the time to take it ahead seriously.

Finances

Financially this month will be slow. The money that is expected could get delayed or stalled for certain reasons and it will require some effort from you to rectify and deal with the challenges. A loan that you have given could turn into bad debt. Do not rush into taking any rash decisions or actions as they would not be much helpful. It is time to stay grounded and steady.

Love

In matters of love, you are likely to receive many opportunities, yet you may find yourself stuck in the past in your head, expecting the worst to happen. It is not necessarily the case with every relationship. If you can get past this, there is a good possibility to invite a loving relationship into your life. For those in a steady relationship, this month you will find much joy and satisfaction in the moments spent with your partner.

Relationships

Relationships can prove to be challenging especially when you are expecting the worst from them. It is a simple matter of perspective this month. While it is not wise to look at the world through rose coloured glasses, at the same time having a bleak perspective is also not the best idea. Don't rush into any judgments or assumptions and give people the benefit of doubt. If you feel you don't have anyone to share your thoughts with, you just need to look harder as there are people willing to be there for you.

Health

Health will be good and on an upward improving trend. Your efforts have been helping and even the tiniest of actions at this time will yield good results. There may be some uncertainty regarding some health symptoms but instead of worrying about them, it is better to get them checked and ruled out for anything serious. Your ideas and plans for your health and lifestyle are good and just need to be implemented with diligence.

Spirituality

This is the time to cut through a lot of thoughts and ideas that seem to not be helping you. You have struggled a lot but all that is in the past and is no longer true. But your mind still believes it and lives with it. It is time to cut through that BS, release any old wounds and patterns and learn to live in a healthier way.

November

Work

Even though opportunities of work abound this month, you may feel as if you get a bad deal or miss out on good things. But the fact is that plenty of good things are happening for you this month. Stuck or delayed work, projects and ventures are likely to move full steam ahead. An offer of promotion or a raise is likely to come to you. Keep your spirits up and stay optimistic. Reach out for help if needed, it is available to you.

Finances

Financially this month will be good but it will have its own lows. Money inflows will be erratic but will be sure to come. Do not over commit to someone as this is not the time to make promises that you may not be able to keep. Do ensure to enjoy some abundance for yourself as well, treat yourself to a gift or a retreat. This is a good time to plan ahead about finances and investments.

Love

Love will be available if only you are willing to take it. Your mood swings sometimes can make it difficult for you to look in the present. Your intuition is working well if only you would listen to it and act upon it. Your personal relationships are undergoing pleasant changes which will become more pronounced as the year ends. Be open to giving and receiving love and don't block the flow in any direction.

Relationships

You will find comfort and pleasure in relationships with friends and family. There is likely to be a reunion or a family get-together. Although it will be a happy time yet it is likely to have its own difficult moments. Do not hold judgments and take things in your stride. It is just a phase. Enjoy the good times. A close friend or family member is willing to help you with your business or financial situation. Be open to the idea.

Health

Health will be average. This month you may see your energy levels go up and down like a roller coaster ride. Remember to keep yourself warm and keep the fires of your passion for life burning. Don't let any negativity and past wounds get in the way. It will be wise this month to reach out to a therapist or a healer to help you deal with any unresolved events or trauma that may be interfering in your health improvement.

Spirituality

It is time to connect to your passion and ignite the drive within you. As you gradually approach your birth month, plenty of things will be happening. This is the time to prepare for them mentally and physically. Practise a ritual, burn candles around you and in your house, do active meditations as that will be more suited to you at this time.

December

Work

Your workplace is going to go through certain changes this month which can feel difficult to deal with initially. But it is just paving way for something better to come that is yet not on the horizon. You may feel let down by certain people who you work with. This is perhaps a sign that it is time to change either your circumstances or the way you work. Again, collaborations will be fruitful. Be open to working with others but be authentic too.

Finances

Financially this will be a good month. The expenses may exceed income but you will be able to handle everything with ease and abundance. This is the right time to learn about investments and savings and how to do it in an efficient manner. You can also explore speculative instruments and if that has been your dream career, invest in learning more about it. Be wise where you spend your money.

Love

Some old relationships or situations are coming to an end. This can be difficult and challenging to deal with but you will soon find the blessings in what happened. It will also be easy for you to deal with any sense of loss or grief. You will find love and support from your partner or a close loved one. You are also in the right mindset to provide loving support to your significant other who may be going through an emotionally tough phase.

Relationships

Relationships will bring you much joy and comfort. There will be happy moments and you will be able to connect better with certain people around you. If you are unsure about someone, listen to your instincts, they will guide you well. Also it may be prudent right now to give yourself and others the benefit of doubt. Many dynamics are shifting within you regarding relationships, so keep an open mind.

Health

Health will be average and you will need to slow down your pace of life to look after it. There is no point trying to address everything as if it were a matter of life and death. Any healing and recovery will take time, so have the patience. It is wise to consult a doctor or an expert to help you deal with a health situation. Do not try to self-medicate or treat yourself.

Spirituality

Life is about give and take. Until both complete each other, the karmic account stays. So if someone has been on your mind negatively or you have felt troubled by them, disconnect with them instead of harbouring any negative thoughts. This will ensure no new karma is created with them and the old one is given a chance to be cleared.

About The Author

Meetu Sehgal is a Tarot Reader, Emotional Wellness Coach, Trainer and Counselling Psychologist.

She is fondly known as "Tarot Healer". With 13+ years of experience in her field, she has been passionately working with individuals helping them resolve health, wealth and relationship challenges through tarot readings, courses and coaching.

She works with people from varied backgrounds, especially with Highly Sensitive People and Empaths and has been helping people heal their emotional baggage, blocks and self-sabotaging patterns to help them create a life of ease, confidence and joy through personal coaching, trainings, EFT, Inner Child Work, NLP, Tarot, Reiki and Angel Therapy.

9 798888 962147

THE ROLE OF ARTIFICIAL INTELLIGENCE IN INDIAN AGRICULTURE: CURRENT SCENARIO AND FUTURE PROSPECTS

SATWIK SAHAY BISARYA | ANIL DHAKAD | PRIYANSH RAHANGDALE